The Knight of the Burning Pestle

THE NEW MERMAIDS

General editor: Brian Gibbons
Professor of English Literature, University of Münster

Previous general editors have been
Philip Brockbank
Brian Morris
Roma Gill

THE NEW MERMAIDS

The Knight of the Burning Pestle

FRANCIS BEAUMONT

Edited by
MICHAEL HATTAWAY
Professor of English Literature
University of Sheffield

LONDON/A & C BLACK

NEW YORK/W W NORTON

Reprinted 1986, 1991, 1993, 1995, 1996
by A & C Black (Publishers) Limited
35 Bedford Row, London WC1R 4JH

First New Mermaid edition 1969
by Ernest Benn Limited
© Ernest Benn Limited 1969

Published in the United States of America
by W. W. Norton & Company Inc.
500 Fifth Avenue, New York, N.Y. 10110

Printed in Great Britain by
Whitstable Litho Printers Ltd, Whitstable, Kent

British Library Cataloguing in Publication Data

Beaumont Francis
  The Knight of the Burning Pestle.—(The new mermaids).
  I. Title   II. Hattaway, Michael   III. Series
  822'.3   PR2427

  ISBN 0-7136-2940-1
  ISBN 0-393-90000-2 (U.S.A.)

CONTENTS

ACKNOWLEDGEMENTS

Anyone who works on *The Knight of the Burning Pestle* must be grateful to H. S. Murch and Cyrus Hoy for their editions of the play. The reader of this text will readily appreciate my debt. My thanks are also due to Dr T. W. Craik and to my colleague Roger Hardy.

M.H.

INTRODUCTION

THE AUTHOR

FRANCIS BEAUMONT was born in 1584 at Grace-Dieu, Leicestershire, the country seat of his family. His grandfather and father had attained distinction as judges, and he evidently intended to continue the family tradition, for, having been admitted as a gentleman commoner of Broadgates Hall (now Pembroke College), Oxford, he left the university in 1600 without taking a degree to become a member of the Inner Temple in London. Like many of his contemporary dramatists, his first publication was an erotic poem, 'Salmacis and Hermaphroditus' (1602). He had probably met Fletcher by 1607 when they both published commendatory verses to Jonson's *Volpone*. In that year too Beaumont published his first play, *The Woman Hater*, a Jonsonian comedy of humours that satirizes the prodigality of the aristocracy. Between 1609 and 1611 the famous partnership with Fletcher was at its height and during these years the King's Men, Shakespeare's company, performed their major collaborative works, *Philaster*, *The Maid's Tragedy*, and *A King and No King*. These plays are in fact the cornerstone of their joint reputation, for although their association is usually taken for granted, Beaumont probably had a hand in only about twelve of the fifty-two plays indiscriminately ascribed to both dramatists by the second folio published in 1679. Fletcher went on writing for the stage alone or in collaboration with others until his death in 1625, but Beaumont seems to have retired from the stage about 1613 when he married Ursula Isley, the co-heiress to a decayed Kentish house. He died on 25 March 1616, the same year as Shakespeare.

AUTHORSHIP AND DATE

Although three of the four seventeenth-century editions of the play attribute *The Knight of the Burning Pestle* to Beaumont and Fletcher, most modern critics, working from the play's unity of conception and from the style of its verse, have ascribed it to Beaumont alone. This ascription is convincingly supported by Cyrus Hoy's analysis of the linguistic habits of the authors who contributed to the Beaumont and Fletcher canon. The relevant evidence and argument, which centres

on the authors' use of 'ye', third person singulars in '-th', and con-
tractions ('i'th', 'h'as', etc.), is set out in two articles: 'The Shares of
Fletcher and his Collaborators in the Beaumont and Fletcher Canon',
(I) and (III), *Studies in Bibliography*, VIII and XI (1956 and 1958),
pp. 129–46 and 85–106.

The first edition of the play is a quarto dated 1613 (Q1). There is
no mention of the author's name on the title-page, nor any indication
of where the play had been performed. The *terminus ad quem* is
therefore 1613, and the *terminus a quo* is 1607, the date of publication
of *The Travels of the Three English Brothers*, the latest of the plays
referred to in the play. In the text the three most important pieces
of evidence for establishing the date more precisely are:

(i) The statements in the publisher's epistle dedicatory that he had
'fostered it privately' in his bosom 'these two years', and that it was
the elder of *Don Quixote* 'above a year'. The first statement would
imply that the play dates from 1611, likewise the second, for Shelton's
translation of Cervantes' novel was entered on the Stationers'
Register on 19 January 1610–11 and published in 1612. In all prob-
ability, however, the publisher, Burre, is referring not to the date of
the first production, but to the date at which Keysar rescued the text
from 'perpetual oblivion'. Keysar presumably provided Burre with a
manuscript of the play sometime *after* it had become clear that the
play would not do well in the theatre. The evidence therefore points
to a date before 1611.

(ii) The Citizen's remark at IV, 49: 'Read the play of *The Four
Prentices of London*, where they toss their pikes so'. The earliest sur-
viving edition of this play is 1615. However, Fleay, in *A Biographical
Chronicle of the English Drama* (London, 1891), i, 182, argues that
the Citizen's reference is to a putative lost edition of 1610, for in the
epistle to the 1615 edition of *The Four Prentices* there is an allusion
to the recent revival of the practice of arms in the Artillery Garden,
a revival which, as Stow's continuator noted, occurred in 1610. Fleay
accordingly dates the play 1610. His argument is, however, based on
evidence which comes only from the epistle, not from that part of the
play which was acted. Moreover, in the same epistle Heywood says
the play was written 'in my infancy of iudgement in this kinde of
poetry . . . some fifteene or sixteene yeares agoe', and an earlier part
of this play, *Godfrey of Bulloigne*, had been entered on the Stationers'
Register as early as 1594. Finally, the context of the Citizen's remark
is ironical, as it suggests that he is treating a play which he had
probably seen but not necessarily read as reliable 'history'.

(iii) The most important evidence, the Citizen's reference to 'this
seven years there hath been plays at this house' (Ind., 6–7), which
would fit almost exactly the years 1600–8 when the Children of the

Queen's Revels were playing at the Blackfriars Theatre before it was taken over by the King's Men in 1609. Moreover, the dedicatee is Robert Keysar, who had managed this troupe from about 1606 (see Irwin Smith, *Shakespeare's Blackfriars Playhouse* [New York, 1964], p. 193).

The weight of the evidence therefore points to an original performance in 1607 or 1608, that is some seven years after the Children of the Revels had moved to Blackfriars. This is confirmed by the Wife's tactless reference to Mulcaster (I, 97), Master of St Paul's, whose troupe was playing at the rival Whitefriars Theatre in 1606–8, and by the reference to the Prince of Moldavia (IV, 57) who was at Court in 1607. The other evidence for dating, the publication of some of Merrythought's songs in 1609, is inconclusive, as these were popular tunes and almost certainly known before their publication. If, however, the later date of 1610–11 is accepted, the play would have been performed at the Whitefriars Theatre where the Children of the Revels (again under Keysar) performed from 1609 to 1614 (see Smith, pp. 194–6).

THE PLAY

If the above argument is correct, *The Knight of the Burning Pestle* was written for the Blackfriars Theatre. This was one of London's private theatres where plays were presented indoors by boy actors to an audience smaller than that of the public theatres and where the price for admission was correspondingly higher. Analysis of the plays presented in the private theatres points to a taste there for elaborate stage effects, for intimate satire, and mannered if not truly sophisticated plays dealing with passionate intrigues of the sort that would appeal to the gentlemen of King James's Court. As John Danby has written of Beaumont and Fletcher, 'the *déclassé* son of the Bishop and the younger son of the Judge are James's unconscious agents. They are capturing the Great House literature for the courtier, writing for adherents of a Stuart King rather than for Tudor aristocrats. Their work, from one point of view, represents a snobbish vulgarisation and a sectional narrowing of the great tradition'.[1] Working from assumptions like these, most critics of *The Knight* have naturally seen the centre of the play in what its first publisher called its 'privy mark of irony',[2] its satire of the merchant class and of the citizens' taste for old-fashioned chivalric romance. Indeed, Alfred Harbage has gone so far as to argue that the play failed at its first presentation

[1] John Danby, *Poets on Fortune's Hill* (London, 1952), p. 157.
[2] See his epistle to Robert Keysar, l. 5.

'not because it satirized citizens, as because it did so without animosity'.[3]

Yet a poem written by Jonson to Fletcher upon *The Faithful Shepherdess* (1608), reminds us that the censorious audience of the Blackfriars was not so homogeneous as to make it easy to argue that any play presented any particular point of view:

> The wise, and many-headed *Bench*, that sits
>   Vpon the Life, and Death of Playes, and Wits,
> (Compos'd of *Gamester, Captaine, Knight, Knight's man,*
>   *Lady*, or *Pusil*, that weares maske, or fan,
> *Veluet*, or *Taffata* cap, rank'd in the darke
>   With the shops *Foreman*, or some such *braue sparke*,
> That may iudge for his *six-pence*) had, before
>   They saw it halfe, damd thy whole play, and more;
> Their motiues were, since it had not to do
>   With vices, which they look'd for, and came to.[4]

Moreover, the play satirizes not only citizens but gallants, not only the militia but the gallery of roués in Barbarossa's cave, as well as the 'gentle' Humphrey, a would-be Paul's man (see V, 50). Satire in fact is incidental to the revelry which informs the play.

It is important to remember how, despite mounting Puritan opposition, holidays and festivals played a large part in Elizabethan life. Many accounts have survived of the descendants of the pagan *saturnalia*, the Feasts of Misrule that took place at Christmas in colleges and great houses when a page or lowly servant would be appointed Boy Bishop or Lord of Misrule to preside over the festivities, of the wanton roisterings of the prentices on Shrove Tuesday (see V, 322), and of the May Day ceremonies, so licentious that they inspired lively descriptions from the pens of Puritan kill-joys.[5] *The Knight of the Burning Pestle* shows signs of having been written for such a festive occasion, possibly May Day when the Wife is making a special visit to the theatre.

The Knight is not Beaumont's first exercise in revelry, for a composition dating from his days at the Inner Temple survives in a manuscript at the British Museum (Sloane, 1709).[6] It is headed

---

[3] A. Harbage, *Shakespeare and the Rival Traditions* (N.Y., 1952), p. 108.

[4] Ben Jonson, *Works*, ed. Herford and Simpson (Oxford, 1925–52), VIII, pp. 370–1. See William A. Armstrong, 'The Audience of the Elizabethan Private Theatres' in G. E. Bentley ed., *The Seventeenth-Century Stage* (Chicago, 1968), pp. 215–34.

[5] See E. K. Chambers, *The Medieval Stage* (London, 1903); C. J. Sisson, *Lost Plays of Shakespeare's Age* (Cambridge, 1936), pp. 157–85; C. L. Barber, *Shakespeare's Festive Comedy* (New York, 1959). Paul Slack ed., *Rebellion, Popular Protest and the Social Order in Early Modern England* (Cambridge, 1984).

[6] It is reprinted by Mark Eccles, 'Francis Beaumont's *Grammar Lecture*', *Review of English Studies*, XVI (1940), pp. 402–14.

I The Blackfriars Theatre, drawn by C. Walter Hodges, based on a
reconstruction by R. Hosley and R. Southern.

'Grammar Lecture' and is a somewhat laborious skit, probably written for a Christmas celebration, that divides the Inn into 'students', 'revelers' ,and 'plodders' and raids the curriculum for its jokes. In our play Rafe's May Lord speech in the interlude between Acts IV and V is no mere exercise in style but sets the pattern for the play.[7] For *The Knight of the Burning Pestle* is a theatrical revel: just as servants at Christmas were permitted to take over a great house for the Feast of Misrule, so here some of the lowlier members of the audience take over the stage. Their taste is not so very undiscriminating—they reject the stock fare offered them and choose instead spectacle and adventure. Rafe might be urged on by the naïve patriotism and city pride of his master and mistress, but he is the hero, is far more likeable than the virtuous Michael and the bullying and heroically sentimental Jasper, and we share his exaltation when he fells the 'giant'. Like Falstaff, who plays his part in a different burlesque of chivalry, he wins as much affection as censure.

Yet satire is of course the staple of the play, and there is no doubt that Beaumont intended some genial fun at the expense of the citizens. In its gentle mocking of general folly the play represents a reaction against the waspish pillorying of individuals which had marked the theatre war that had raged at the turn of the century. The portrayal of the citizens' over-blown pride in their craft, city, and country is a parody of the uncritical patriotism celebrated in plays from the public theatres, plays like Dekker's *The Shoemakers' Holiday* (c. 1599), and the plays listed in the Induction (ll. 19ff). The chatter of the Citizen and his Wife, their terms of endearment, their bawdy, their ignorance of the classics, and the Wife's trust in homely medicines are easily guyed. More important, though, is their theatrical naïveté. Like the rustics in *A Midsummer Night's Dream* (see I.ii), their taste is for 'huffing' parts, for bombast, romance, and spectacle. But our response to them as to Rafe is not merely critical, for they thoroughly enjoy the play, are caught up in it to such a degree that they forget it is art. Their reactions are really a rebuke to the academics, to opinions like those of Sir Philip Sidney who, by maintaining the classical principles of decorum and verisimilitude, was also trying to compound art with nature. Complaining of the disregard of the unities in romance plays, he wrote about 1581:

> You shall haue *Asia* of the one side, and *Affricke* of the other, and so manie other vnder Kingdomes, that the Player when he comes in, must euer begin with telling where he is, or else the tale will not be conceiued. Now you shall haue three ladies walke to gather flowers, and then we must beleeue the stage to be a garden. By and by we heare newes of shipwrack in the same place, then we are too blame

[7] Old Merrythought claims his wife and son have been a-Maying, V. 226.

if we accept it not for a Rock. Vpon the back of that, comes out a hidious monster with fire and smoke, and then the miserable beholders are bound to take it for a Caue: while in the meane time two Armies flie in, represented with foure swords and bucklers, and thé what hard hart wil not receiue it for a pitched field.[8]

The citizens display their naïveté notably in their comments on 'The London Merchant', the play they had come to see. The interest of it lies in the contest for Luce's hand between the 'gentle' but stupid Humphrey and the 'prodigal' apprentice Jasper. In that Jasper eventually wins the maiden, the play inverts the usual pattern of plays depicting prodigals (see Luke, xv, 11–32); in fact it parodies plays like Dekker's *Old Fortunatus* (1599) and the anonymous *The London Prodigal* (1604) where the wayward son usually repents of his ways.[9] The gullible Citizen and his Wife of course side with Humphrey, nor do they realize that the prudent Venturewell who would 'venture' his daughter in marriage with this gentleman represents the more unattractive qualities of their own class. The other main character in this play, Merrythought, is a Jonsonian humour, a satirical version of the type best known to us in Dekker's Simon Eyre from *The Shoemakers' Holiday*. Yet by making his wife capitulate and join in his revelry he wins a victory for life and nature over the customary and mercenary values of business society.

But it is the citizens' taste for romance which is the main object of the play's satire. Their appetite for it is voracious: they know not only Spenser (see II, 168 and III, 426) and the old tales of Guy of Warwick (see II, 511) and Bevis of Hampton (see III, 108),[10] but have devoured the interminable Iberian prose romances that were being industriously translated at this time: *Palmerin d'Oliva* and its sequel *Palmerin of England*; Ortuñez de Calahorra's *Espejo de Principes y Caualleros*, translated as *The Mirror of Knighthood*; and *Amadis de Gaul*. In this last there appears a Knight of the Burning Sword, who was probably the original of the Knight of the Burning Pestle with its obvious phallic references.[11] The title also relates to a number of

[8] Sir Philip Sidney, *Works*, ed. A. Feuillerat (Cambridge, 1912), iii, 38.
[9] See John Doebler, 'Beaumont's *The Knight of the Burning Pestle* and the Prodigal Son Plays', *Studies in English Literature*, V (1965), pp. 333–44; and B. Maxwell, '*The Knight of the Burning Pestle* and *Wily Beguiled*', in *Studies in Beaumont, Fletcher, and Massinger* (Chapel Hill, 1939), pp. 14–16.
[10] See R. S. Crane, *The Vogue of the Medieval Chivalric Romance during the Renaissance* (Menasta, Wisc., 1919).
[11] The Knight of the Burning Sword is also mentioned in *Don Quixote*, tr. Shelton (London, 1901), i, pp. 4 and 154; and cf. *1 Henry IV*, III, iii, 27 where Falstaff calls Bardolph 'The Knight of the Burning Lamp'—with reference to his nose. Burning probably means 'gilded'—it also refers to the effects of syphilis.

Elpejo de Principes y Caualleros, en el qual, en tres libros, se cuentan los immortales hechos del Cauallero del Febo, y de su hermano Rosicler, hijos del grã-de Emperador Trebacio. Con las altas cauallerias, y muy e-straños amores dela muy hermosa y estremada Princesa Claridiana, y de otros altos Principes y Caualleros.

DIRIGIDO AL MVY ILLVSTRE
Señor don Martin Cortes, Marques del Valle. Por Diego Ortuñez de Calahorra, de la ciudad de Nagera.
CON PRIVILEGIO.
En Medina del Campo, Por Francisco del Canto. M. D. LXXXIII.

A costa de Iuan Boyer, Mercader de libros.

II   The title-page of Ortuñez de Calahorra's *Espejo de Principes y Caualleros* (*The Mirror of Knighthood*)

heroical romance plays performed at Court in the 1570s and 1580s, among which was a play, now lost, called *The Knight of the Burning Rock*.[12] The accounts of the office of the Revels reveal how these plays must have relied largely on spectacular productions for their effect.[13] Romantic dramas had also been performed later at the public theatres; among this group are plays like Greene's *Orlando Furioso* (1591-2), Dekker's *Old Fortunatus* (1599), both played at the Rose, and three of the plays mentioned by Beaumont: the immensely popular *Mucedorus* (1588, see Ind. 83), Heywood's *The Four Prentices of London* (1600, see IV, 49) and Day, Rowley, and Wilkins's *The Travels of the Three English Brothers*[14] (1607, see IV, 29) which lace their accounts of fabulous adventure with patriotic sentiment.

Beaumont was not the first to parody plays of this type—indeed the tradition of romance blended with wit goes back at least as far as Chaucer's *Sir Thopas*. Elizabethan scholars like Sidney, Puttenham,[15] and later Jonson[16] had mocked the common people's love of this literature that rested so firmly on the chivalric virtues of honour and constancy, virtues with which the bourgeois Jasper is infected when he would test Luce's love (see III, 72). Peele and Nashe too had burlesqued the extravagance of heroical adventure: in *The Old Wife's Tale* (1590), like *The Knight of the Burning Pestle* set within a framework of revelry with pages called Antic, Frolic, and Fantastic, Peele crams wandering knights, evil magicians, and damsels in distress into about an hour's entertainment; and Nashe's prose narrative *The Unfortunate Traveller* (1594) shows a youth in search of fabulous adventure. These plays, together with the plays satirizing the citizens themselves, too numerous to list here but including the great comedies of Jonson and Middleton, are as important to *The Knight of the Burning Pestle* as Cervantes' *Don Quixote*. Obviously, Beaumont knew the greatest of the Renaissance romance parodies,[17] shared Cervantes' attitude towards the Iberian romances, and imitated his kindly ironic treatment of the hero. He also borrowed at least the Innkeeper episode for his play. But one should not stress Beaumont's debt to Cervantes too much as *The Knight* is basically an accumulation of

---

[12] See Alfred Harbage, *Annals of English Drama* (London, 1964), pp. 40ff., and L. M. Ellison, *The Early Romantic Drama at the English Court* (Chicago, 1917).

[13] A. Feuillerat, *Documents Relating to the Office of the Revels in the Time of Elizabeth* (Louvain, 1908), *passim*.

[14] In this play one of the prentices takes a pestle as his emblem.

[15] G. Puttenham, *The Arte of English Poesie*, ed. G. D. Willcock and A. Walker (Cambridge, 1936), p. 83.

[16] See *The Magnetic Lady*, *Works*, vi, 527-8, etc.

[17] The Inn Scene derives from *Don Quixote*, I. ii.

El cauallero del Febo:

SEGVNDA PARTE DE ESPE-
IO DE PRINCIPES Y CAVALLEROS, DIVI-
dida en dos libros: donde se trata de los altos hechos
del Emperador Trebacio, y de sus caros hijos, el gran Alphebo, e incli
to Rosicler, y del muy excelente Claridiano, hijo del cauallero del Febo, y de la Emperatriz Claridiana: y assi mismo de Poliphebo de Tina
cria, y de la excelentissima Archisilora Reyna de Lira, y de otros
muy altos Principes Compuesto por Pedro de la Sierra,
Infançon, natural de Cariñena, en el
Reyno de Aragon.

CON PRIVILEGIO.

En Valladolid, en casa de Diego Fernandez de Cordoua.
Año de M. D. LXXXV.

III   From the *Espejo*

conventional episodes from romances and English plays as well as of elements from a native tradition of satire all of which are welded into a splendid entertainment. Source spotting in fact brings comparatively little reward, for Beaumont has transmuted his materials, and his sheer capacity for style, his ability to produce mock-heroic pentameters for Rafe, competent verse for the lovers, lively prose for the citizens, pompous couplets for Humphrey, to compose songs and collect ballads, has made this a virtuoso play. This is no mere parody, but shows an acute awareness of a society that was rapidly changing, and is a record of a world well lost. [18]

---

[18] The most notable modern professional production of the play was that of Michael Bogdanov for the Royal Shakespeare Company which opened on 10 April, 1981.

NOTE ON THE TEXT

The Knight of the Burning Pestle was first printed in a quarto dated 1613. It (Q1) was published by Walter Burre, and W. W. Greg showed that it was printed by Nicholas Okes. Two further quartos are dated 1635: the first of these (Q2) was also printed by Okes for a new publisher, 'I.S.' (John Spencer). It was set up from Q1 and adds an epistle, a prologue taken from Lyly's *Sapho and Phao*, as well as a *Dramatis Personae*. The second (Q3), which can be distinguished by its spelling 'Beamount' on the title page, contains many changes in spelling conventions which suggest that it was printed some years later, some time before the appearance of the second Beaumont and Fletcher folio in 1679. *The Knight* is one of the plays excluded from the folio of 1647 but it was reprinted from Q3 in the second folio (F).

Apart from some mislineation the text supplies few difficulties. The literary and inaccurate stage directions of Q1 suggest that the text derives from the author's manuscript,[18] each of the early editions derives from its immediate predecessor, and no important changes occur.

This text is based upon the British Museum copy (C.34.f.30) of Q1, collated with the British Museum copies of Q2, Q3, and F. It incorporates the press corrections made in that edition as well as some readings from the later editions. (A variorum text with full bibliographical apparatus is provided by Cyrus Hoy in Volume I of *The Dramatic Works in the Beaumont and Fletcher Canon* edited by Fredson Bowers [Cambridge, 1966].) Like the seventeenth-century editions, the present text is divided into acts and interludes, but not scenes, as the action is linked together by the continuing presence on the stage of the Citizen and his Wife. Their comments have been divided from the main body of the text by a double space to aid comprehension. As with all New Mermaid texts, spelling and punctuation have been modernized, abbreviations silently expanded, speech prefixes regularized, songs separated from the text and italicized, and all substantive departures from Q1 noted in the glossary. The music for the songs has not been reprinted as only a portion is extant, and many tunes associated with Merrythought's ballads are not contemporary with the play. However, references are given to reliable transcripts.

[18] See W. T. Jewkes, *Act Division in Elizabethan and Jacobean Plays, 1583–1616* (Hamden, Conn., 1958).

ABBREVIATIONS

Bradbrook = M. C. Bradbrook, *The Growth and Structure of Elizabethan Comedy* (London, 1955).

Brand = J. Brand, *Faiths and Folklore* (an edition of *The Popular Antiquities of Great Britain*), ed. W. C. Hazlitt, 2 vols. (London 1905).

Bronson = B. H. Bronson, *The Traditional Tunes of the Child Ballads* (Princeton, 1959–).

Chappell = William Chappell, *Old English Popular Music*, ed. H. E. Wooldridge, 2 vols. (London, 1893).

Dyce = Alexander Dyce ed., *The Works of Beaumont and Fletcher*, 11 vols. (London, 1843–6).

F = The second folio text of 1679.

Gurr = A. J. Gurr ed., *The Knight of the Burning Pestle* (Edinburgh, 1968).

Harbage = Alfred Harbage, *Shakespeare and the Rival Traditions* (New York, 1952).

Hoy = Cyrus Hoy's edition of *The Knight of the Burning Pestle*, in Vol. I of *The Dramatic Works in the Beaumont and Fletcher Canon*, general editor Fredson Bowers (Cambridge, 1966–).

M L N = Modern Language Notes.

Murch = H. S. Murch ed., *The Knight of the Burning Pestle*, Yale Studies in English, XXXIII (New York, 1908).

Partridge = Eric Partridge, *Shakespeare's Bawdy* (London, 1947).

Q1 = The first quarto of 1613.

Q1^c = Corrected copy of Q1.

Q1^u = Uncorrected copy of Q1.

Q2 = The second quarto of 1635.

Q3 = The third quarto (falsely dated 1635).

s. d. = Stage direction.

s. p. = Speech prefix.

S P = Studies in Philology.

Smith = Irwin Smith, *Shakespeare's Blackfriars Playhouse* (New York, 1964).

Stow = John Stow, *A Survey of London*, ed. C. L. Kingsford, 2 vols. (Oxford, 1908).

Stubbes = Philip Stubbes, *The Anatomie of Abuses*, ed. F. J. Furnivall, 2 vols. (London, 1877–92).

Sugden = Edward Sugden, *A Topographical Dictionary to the Works of Shakespeare and his Contemporaries* (Manchester, 1925).

Tilley = M. P. Tilley, *A Dictionary of the Proverbs in England in the Sixteenth and Seventeenth Centuries* (Ann Arbor, 1950).

FURTHER READING

The standard complete edition of Beaumont and Fletcher is edited by Arnold Glover and A. R. Waller, 10 vols. (Cambridge, 1905-12), although it will soon be supplanted by the Cambridge edition under the general editorship of Fredson Bowers. Modern editions of *The Knight* include those edited by R. M. Alden, in the Belles-Lettres Series (Boston, 1910), Cyrus Hoy (old spelling) in Volume 1 of *The Dramatic Works in the Beaumont and Fletcher Canon* (Cambridge 1966), John Doebler in the Regents Renaissance Drama Series (London, 1967), and Sheldon Zitner in the Revels Plays (Manchester, 1985). Useful material will also be found in:

W. W. Appleton, *Beaumont and Fletcher, a Critical Study* (London, 1956) .

Lee Bliss, *Francis Beaumont* (Boston, 1987).

—'*Don Quixote* in England: the Case for *The Knight of the Burning Pestle*', *Viator*, XVIII (1987), pp.361–80.

—' "Plot me no Plots": the Life of Drama and the Drama of Life in *The Knight of the Burning Pestle*', *Modern Language Quarterly*, XLV (1984), pp.3–21.

Michael D. Bristol, *Carnival and Theater* (New York, 1985).

Ann J. Cook, *The Privileged Playgoers of Shakespeare's London 1576–1642* (Princeton, N.J., 1981).

J. F. Danby, *Poets on Fortune's Hill* (London, 1952).

J. W. Doebler, 'Francis Beaumont's *The Knight of the Burning Pestle*', unpublished Ph. D. dissertation, University of Wisconsin, 1961.

Brian Gibbons, *Jacobean City Comedy* (London, 1968).

Andrew Gurr, *The Shakespearean Stage, 1574–1642* (Cambridge, 1970).

Michael Hattaway, *Elizabethan Popular Theatre* (London, 1982).

Richard Hosley, 'A Reconstruction of the Second Blackfriars' in David Galloway ed., *The Elizabethan Theatre I* (Hamden, Conn., 1970).

Pierre Iselin (ed.), *F. Beaumont and J. Fletcher: The Knight of the Burning Pestle* (Didier Erudition, Paris, 1996).

Arthur C. Kirsch, *Jacobean Dramatic Perspectives* (Charlottesville, 1972).

Clifford Leech, *The John Fletcher Plays* (London, 1962).

Inge Leimberg, 'Das Spiel mit der dramatischen Illusion in Beaumonts *The Knight of the Burning Pestle*', *Anglia*, LXXXI (1962), pp. 142–74.

E. S. Lindsey, 'The Original Music for *The Knight of the Burning Pestle*', *S P*, XXVI (1929), pp. 425–43.

Ronald F. Miller, 'Dramatic Form and Dramatic Imagination in Beaumont's *The Knight of the Burning Pestle*', *English Literary Renaissance*, VIII (1978), pp. 67–84.

E. H. C Oliphant, *The Plays of Beaumont and Fletcher* (New Haven, 1927).

Laurie E. Osborne, 'Female audiences and female authority in *The Knight of the Burning Pestle*', *Exemplaria*, III (1991), pp.491–517.

E. C. Pettet, *Shakespeare and the Romance Tradition* (London, 1949).

David H. Samuelson, 'The Order in Beaumont's *Knight of the Burning Pestle*', *English Literary Renaissance*, IX (1979), pp. 302–18.

Michael Shapiro, *Children of the Revels: the Boy Companies of Shakespeare's Time and their Plays* (New York, 1977).

A. C. Sprague, *Beaumont and Fletcher on the Restoration Stage* (Cambridge, Mass., 1926).

Glenn A. Steinberg, ' "You know the plot/We both agreed on?": plot self-consciousness, and *The London Merchant* in *The Knight of the Burning Pestle*', *Medieval and Renaissance Drama in England*, V (1991), pp.211–24.

S. Tannenbaum, *Beaumont and Fletcher, a Concise Bibliography* (New York, 1928).

A. H. Thorndike, *The Influence of Beaumont and Fletcher on Shakespeare* (Worcester, Mass., 1901).

Eugene M. Waith, *The Pattern of Tragicomedy in Beaumont and Fletcher* (New Haven, 1952).

Lawrence B. Wallis, *Fletcher, Beaumont and Company* (New York, 1947).

Robert Weimann, *Shakespeare and the Popular Tradition in the Theatre* (London, 1978).

THE
KNIGHT OF
the Burning Pestle.

——————————— *Quod si*
Iudicium subtile, videndis artibus illud
Ad libros & ad hæc Musarum dona vocares:
Bæotum in crasso iurares aëre natos.
Horat. in Epist. ad Oct. Aug.

Aut prodesse solent aut delectare poeta.

LONDON,

Printed for *walter Burre*, and are to be sold at the
signe of the Crane in Paules Church-yard.
1613.

TO HIS MANY WAYS ENDEARED
FRIEND MASTER ROBERT KEYSAR

Sir, this unfortunate child who in eight days (as lately I have
learned) was begot and born, soon after was by his parents
(perhaps because he was so unlike his brethren) exposed to the
wide world, who for want of judgement, or not understanding the
privy mark of irony about it (which showed it was no offspring   5
of any vulgar brain) utterly rejected it; so that for want of ac-
ceptance it was even ready to give up the ghost, and was in danger to have been smothered in perpetual oblivion, if you (out of
your direct antipathy to ingratitude) had not been moved both
to relieve and cherish it. Wherein I must needs commend both   10
your judgement, understanding, and singular love to good wits.
You afterwards sent it to me, yet being an infant and somewhat
ragged; I have fostered it privately in my bosom these two
years, and now to show my love return it to you, clad in good
lasting clothes, which scarce memory will wear out, and able to   15
speak for itself; and, withal, as it telleth me, desirous to try his
fortune in the world, where if yet it be welcome, father, foster-
father, nurse, and child, all have their desired end. If it be
slighted or traduced, it hopes his father will beget him a
younger brother who shall revenge his quarrel, and challenge   20
the world either of fond and merely literal interpretation, or
illiterate misprision. Perhaps it will be thought to be of the race
of *Don Quixote*: we both may confidently swear it is his elder
above a year; and therefore may (by virtue of his birthright)

2 *his parents.* Would suggest joint authorship were it not for 'father' in
l. 17.
5–6 *no offspring of any vulgar brain.* Not an ordinary citizen comedy.
6 *rejected it.* Either the author did not get his play performed or it was
not well received.
12–13 *somewhat ragged.* The author's foul papers.
17–18 *father . . . child.* Author, dedicatee, publisher, and play.

ROBERT KEYSAR. A wealthy London goldsmith who had financed the Children
of the Revels at the Blackfriars Theatre from about 1606 (see Smith,
pp. 193 ff.).
23 *Don Quixote.* Shelton's translation of Cervantes' parody was published
in 1612, but both the translation and the original (1605) had circulated
before then.

3

challenge the wall of him. I doubt not but they will meet   25
in their adventures, and I hope the breaking of one staff will
make them friends; and perhaps they will combine themselves,
and travel through the world to seek their adventures. So I
commit him to his good fortune, and myself to your love.

Your assured friend W.B.   30

25 *challenge the wall of him* demand the safest part of the footpath,
   hence claim precedence

---

26 *breaking of one staff*. Possibly the barber's pole (see III, 332 s.d.)—an
   incident borrowed from Cervantes.
30 *W.B.* Walter Burre, the publisher.

TO THE READERS OF THIS COMEDY

Gentlemen, the world is so nice in these our times, that for
apparel, there is no fashion; for music, which is a rare art
(though now slighted), no instrument; for diet, none but the
French kickshaws that are delicate; and for plays, no invention
but that which now runneth an invective way, touching some   5
particular person, or else it is contemned before it is throughly
understood. This is all that I have to say, that the author had no
intent to wrong anyone in this comedy, but as a merry passage,
here and there interlaced it with delight, which he hopes will
please all, and be hurtful to none.   10

TO THE READERS from Q2 (om. Q1)
  1 *nice* fastidious
  4 *kickshaws* <Fr. *quelque chose*, insubstantial dainties
  6 *throughly* thoroughly

THE PROLOGUE

Where the bee can suck no honey, she leaves her sting behind;
and where the bear cannot find origanum to heal his grief, he
blasteth all other leaves with his breath. We fear it is like to fare
so with us, that seeing you cannot draw from our labours sweet
content, you leave behind you a sour mislike and with open   5
reproach blame our good meaning because you cannot reap the
wonted mirth. Our intent was at this time to move inward
delight, not outward lightness; and to breed (if it might be) soft
smiling, not loud laughing, knowing it to the wise to be as great
pleasure to hear counsel mixed with wit, as to the foolish to   10
have sport mingled with rudeness. They were banished the
theatre of Athens, and from Rome hissed, that brought
parasites on the stage with apish actions, or fools with uncivil
habits, or courtezans with immodest words. We have en-
deavoured to be as far from unseemly speeches to make your   15
ears glow, as we hope you will be free from unkind reports, or,
mistaking the author's intention (who never aimed at any one
particular in this play), to make our cheeks blush. And thus I
leave it and thee to thine own censure, to like, or dislike. *Vale.*

PROLOGUE from Q2, where it is reprinted from Lyly's *Sapho and Phao*
    (1584), (om. Q1)
  2 *origanum* herb from majoram family
  9 *as great* ed. a great Q2
 13 *parasites* 'men that frequent rich tables and obtain their welcome
    by flattery' (Johnson)
 19 *Vale* farewell

THE SPEAKERS' NAMES

The Prologue
Then a Citizen
The Citizen's Wife, and
Rafe, her man, sitting below
   amidst the spectators
[Venturewell], a rich mer-
   chant
Jasper, his apprentice
Master Humphrey, a friend
   to the merchant
Luce, the merchant's
   daughter
Mistress Merrythought, Jas-
   per's mother
Michael, a second son of
   Mistress Merrythought
Old Master Merrythought

[Tim], a squire   ⎱ [Appren-
[George], a dwarf ⎰ tices]
A Tapster
A Boy that danceth and
   singeth   5
An Host
A Barber
[Three Captive] Knights
[A Captive Woman]
A Sergeant   10
Soldiers
[Boys
William Hamerton, a pew-
   terer
George Greengoose, a   15
   poulterer
Pompiona, daughter to the
   King of Moldavia]

THE SPEAKERS' NAMES from Q2 (om. Q1)
  8 [*Three Captive*] *Knights* ed. Two Knights Q2
  8–10 Q2–3, F list *A Captaine* between *Knights* and *A Sergeant*; this
     must refer to Rafe in the Mile End scene (V, 87 ff.)
  11 *the* F (om.Q2)

THE FAMOUS HISTORY OF
THE KNIGHT OF THE BURNING PESTLE

[Induction

GENTLEMEN *seated upon the stage. The* CITIZEN, *his* WIFE, *and*
RAFE *below among the audience.*]

Enter PROLOGUE

[PROLOGUE]

    From all that's near the court, from all that's great
    Within the compass of the city-walls,
    We now have brought our scene—

Enter CITIZEN [*from audience below*]

CITIZEN

    Hold your peace, goodman boy.

PROLOGUE

    What do you mean, sir?   5

CITIZEN

    That you have no good meaning. This seven years there hath
    been plays at this house, I have observed it, you have still
    girds at citizens; and now you call your play *The London*
    Merchant. Down with your title, boy, down with your title!

PROLOGUE

    Are you a member of the noble city?   10

CITIZEN

    I am.

PROLOGUE

    And a freeman?

---

  7 *still* always   8 *girds* sneers
 10 *member* inhabitant

---

s.d. GENTLEMEN. The behaviour of the tobacco smoking gallants who paid
    for stools on the stage itself is satirized in Beaumont's *The Woman Hater*
    (I. iii), Dekker's *The Gull's Hornbook* (Ch. iii.), and in plays by Jonson.
s.d. PROLOGUE. Wore a long black velvet cloak and a garland of bays.
  6–7 *seven . . . house.* The Children of the Queen's Revels played at Black-
    friars from 1600 to 1608.
  8–9 *The London Merchant.* Possibly a lost play by Ford, but more probably
    the name of the play dealing with Venturewell and his family.
  9 *title.* A placard bearing the name of the play hung on the stage.
 12 *freeman.* Enjoying the privileges of the City; admission to the rank
    came after serving a term of apprenticeship.

11

CITIZEN
   Yea, and a grocer.

PROLOGUE
   So, grocer, then by your sweet favour, we intend no abuse to
the city.   15

CITIZEN
   No, sir? Yes, sir! If you were not resolved to play the jacks,
what need you study for new subjects, purposely to abuse
your betters? Why could not you be contented, as well as
others, with *The Legend of Whittington*, or *The Life and
Death of Sir Thomas Gresham, with the Building of the Royal*   20
Exchange, or *The Story of Queen Elenor, with the Rearing of
London Bridge upon Wool-sacks?*

PROLOGUE
   You seem to be an understanding man. What would you have
us do, sir?

CITIZEN
   Why, present something notably in honour of the commons   25
of the city.

PROLOGUE
   Why, what do you say to *The Life and Death of Fat Drake,
or the Repairing of Fleet-privies*?

CITIZEN
   I do not like that; but I will have a citizen, and he shall be of
my own trade.   30

---

14 *favour* pun on *favour* as 'face'
16 *play the jacks* play the knave, do a mean trick (Tilley, J8)
23 *understanding* pun since the spectators were below the stage; cf.
   Bartholomew Fair, Induction, 'the understanding gentlemen o'
   the ground'
25 *commons* the body of freemen

---

13 *grocer*. A member of one of the most important of the twelve great
   livery companies of London.
19ff. Plays from public theatres that glorified the City: Dick Whittington
   was the legendary Lord Mayor who rose from low estate to great
   fortune, a play about him was entered on the Stationers' Register in
   1605; Sir Thomas Gresham appears in Part II of Heywood's *If You
   Know Not Me* printed in 1606, he had built the Royal Exchange, a cos-
   mopolitan place of resort that was destroyed in the fire of 1666; Queen
   Elenor is probably from Peele's *Edward I* printed in 1593; 'The
   Building of London Bridge upon Wool Packs' was the name of a dance
   that got its name from a levy upon wool raised to pay for the bridge.
27 *Fat Drake*. Probably a sarcastic invention of the Prologue.
28 *Fleet-privies*. Fleet Ditch served as a sewer.

PROLOGUE

Oh, you should have told us your mind a month since. Our
play is ready to begin now.

CITIZEN

'Tis all one for that; I will have a grocer, and he shall do
admirable things.

PROLOGUE

What will you have him do?   35

CITIZEN

Marry, I will have him—

WIFE *below*

WIFE

Husband, husband.

RAFE *below*

RAFE

Peace, mistress.

WIFE

Hold thy peace, Rafe; I know what I do, I warrant'ee.—
Husband, husband.   40

CITIZEN

What say'st thou, cony?

WIFE

Let him kill a lion with a pestle, husband; let him kill a lion
with a pestle.

CITIZEN

So he shall.—I'll have him kill a lion with a pestle.

WIFE

Husband, shall I come up, husband?   45

---

34 *admirable* wonderful
41 *cony* rabbit, term of endearment

31–2 *Our play is ready to begin now.* The players were in fact accustomed to
  demands for a change in the programme; see Bradbrook, pp. 24–5.
41 *cony* cf. Chapman, *The Blind Beggar of Alexandria* (1595), V. 37–9:

> New-fashion terms I like not, for a man
> To call his wife cony, forsooth and lamb:
> And pork and mutton, he as well may say.

42 *kill a lion with a pestle.* Battles with wild beasts were common in the
  romances and one of the prentices in Heywood's *The Four Prentices of
  London* claims to have killed a lion single-handed.
45 *shall I come up.* For a woman to sit on the stage was both unusual and
  immodest.

CITIZEN

Ay, cony.—Rafe, help your mistress this way.—Pray,
gentlemen, make her a little room.—I pray you, sir, lend me
your hand to help up my wife; I thank you, sir.—So.

[WIFE *comes up onto stage*]

WIFE

By your leave, gentlemen all, I'm something troublesome;
I'm a stranger here; I was ne'er at one of these plays, as they   50
say, before; but I should have seen *Jane Shore* once, and my
husband hath promised me any time this twelvemonth to
carry me to *The Bold Beauchamps*; but in truth he did not.
I pray you bear with me.

CITIZEN

Boy, let my wife and I have a couple of stools, and then   55
begin, and let the grocer do rare things.

PROLOGUE

But sir, we have never a boy to play him; everyone hath a
part already.

WIFE

Husband, husband, for God's sake let Rafe play him;
beshrew me if I do not think he will go beyond them all.   60

CITIZEN

Well remembered, wife.—Come up, Rafe.—I'll tell you,
gentlemen, let them but lend him a suit of reparel and
necessaries, and, by gad, if any of them all blow wind in the
tail on him, I'll be hanged.

[RAFE *comes up onto stage*]

WIFE

I pray you, youth, let him have a suit of reparel.—I'll be   65
sworn, gentlemen, my husband tells you true: he will act
you sometimes at our house, that all the neighbours cry out
on him. He will fetch you up a couraging part so in the

55 *of* Q2 (om. Q1)
60 *beshrew me* the devil take me
62 *reparel* archaic synonym for apparel
63–4 *blow wind in the tail on* come near (from horseracing)
67–8 *cry out on* complain of
68 *couraging* spirited

---

51 *Jane Shore*. Also a citizen's wife and a mistress of Edward IV, she
appears in Heywood's *Edward IV* printed in 1600; there are references in Henslowe's *Diary* to plays about her composed by Chettle
and Day.
53 *The Bold Beauchamps*. A lost play ascribed to Heywood.

garret, that we are all as feared, I warrant you, that we quake
again. We'll fear our children with him: if they be never so   70
unruly, do but cry, 'Rafe comes, Rafe comes', to them, and
they'll be as quiet as lambs.—Hold up thy head, Rafe; show
the gentlemen what thou canst do; speak a huffing part; I
warrant you the gentlemen will accept of it.

CITIZEN

Do, Rafe, do.   75

RAFE

By heaven, methinks it were an easy leap
To pluck bright honour from the pale-faced moon,
Or dive into the bottom of the sea,
Where never fathom line touched any ground,
And pluck up drowned honour from the lake of hell.   80

CITIZEN

How say you, gentlemen, is it not as I told you?

WIFE

Nay, gentlemen, he hath played before, my husband says,
Mucedorus before the wardens of our company.

CITIZEN

Ay, and he should have played Jeronimo with a shoemaker
for a wager.   85

PROLOGUE

He shall have a suit of apparel if he will go in.

CITIZEN

In, Rafe; in, Rafe; and set out the grocery in their kind, if
thou lov'st me.   [*Exit* RAFE]

WIFE

I warrant our Rafe will look finely when he's dressed.

---

73 *huffing* puffed up, bombastic
87 *in their kind* fittingly

76ff. *By heaven . . . lake of hell.* Hotspur's speech in *1 Henry IV*, I. iii,
    201 ff., a fine bombastic or huffing part; Rafe substitutes a common-
    place 'from the lake of hell' for Shakespeare's 'by the locks'.
83 *Mucedorus.* A very popular and absurdly extravagant play first printed
    anonymously in 1598 in which scenes of romantic adventure are laced
    with buffoonery.
83 *before the wardens.* Performances by livery companies in the Guildhalls
    and at Court (cf. *A Midsummer Night's Dream*) continued throughout
    the first half of the seventeenth century.
84 *Jeronimo.* The hero of Kyd's *The Spanish Tragedy.*
86 *go in.* To the tiring-house behind the stage.
87 *in their kind.* Each company had a distinctive livery.

PROLOGUE
   But what will you have it called?   90
CITIZEN
   The Grocers' Honour.
PROLOGUE
   Methinks *The Knight of the Burning Pestle* were better.
WIFE
   I'll be sworn, husband, that's as good a name as can be.
CITIZEN
   Let it be so. Begin, begin; my wife and I will sit down.
PROLOGUE
   I pray you, do.   95
CITIZEN
   What stately music have you? You have shawms?
PROLOGUE
   Shawms? No.
CITIZEN
   No? I'm a thief if my mind did not give me so. Rafe plays a
   stately part, and he must needs have shawms; I'll be at the
   charge of them myself, rather than we'll be without them.   100
PROLOGUE
   So you are like to be.
CITIZEN
   Why, and so I will be. There's two shillings; let's have the
   waits of Southwark. They are as rare fellows as any are in
   England; and that will fetch them all o'er the water with a
   vengeance, as if they were mad.   105
PROLOGUE
   You shall have them. Will you sit down then?
CITIZEN
   Ay.—Come, wife.
WIFE
   Sit you merry all, gentlemen. I'm bold to sit amongst you for
   my ease.

---

92 *Burning* gilded (see II, 296)
96 *shawms* forerunners of oboes
103 *waits* band of wind-instrument players maintained by City at
   public expense

---

92 *The Knight of the Burning Pestle.* See Introduction, p. xv.
104 *o'er the water.* The Borough of Southwark is across the river from the
   City where the theatre was; 'two shillings would have been a fair day's
   wage, though not enough to make them enthusiastic' (Gurr).

PROLOGUE
From all that's near the court, from all that's great   110
Within the compass of the city-walls,
We now have brought our scene. Fly far from hence
All private taxes, immodest phrases,
Whate'er may but show like vicious:
For wicked mirth never true pleasure brings,   115
But honest minds are pleased with honest things.
—Thus much for that we do; but for Rafe's part you must
answer for yourself.   [*Exit*]

CITIZEN
Take you no care for Rafe; he'll discharge himself, I warrant
you.   120

WIFE
I' faith, gentlemen, I'll give my word for Rafe.

[Act I]

Enter MERCHANT [*i.e.* VENTUREWELL] *and* JASPER, *his prentice*

MERCHANT
Sirrah, I'll make you know you are my prentice,
And whom my charitable love redeemed
Even from the fall of fortune; gave thee heat
And growth to be what now thou art, new cast thee;
Adding the trust of all I have at home,   5
In foreign staples, or upon the sea,
To thy direction; tied the good opinions
Both of myself and friends to thy endeavours:
So fair were thy beginnings. But with these,
As I remember, you had never charge   '   10
To love your master's daughter, and even then
When I had found a wealthy husband for her.

117–18 *you . . . yourself* printed as verse in Q1
119 *discharge himself* acquit himself, also ejaculate (see Partridge)
    Act I ed. Actus primi, Scœna prima Q1
3–4 *heat And growth* shelter and sustenance
4 *new cast thee* formed you again
6 *staples* centres of commerce, or storehouses
11 *even* especially

---

113 *private taxes.* Possibly a reference to the personal satires used as weapons
in the War of the Theatres (see Bradbrook, pp. 103 ff. and Harbage,
pp. 90 ff.); like Jonson, Beaumont thought that the satiric function of
drama was to correct general folly and vice and not particular persons;
cf. the prologue to *The Woman Hater.*

I take it, sir, you had not; but, however,
I'll break the neck of that commission
And make you know you are but a merchant's factor.   15

JASPER

Sir, I do liberally confess I am yours,
Bound both by love and duty to your service,
In which my labour hath been all my profit.
I have not lost in bargain, nor delighted
To wear your honest gains upon my back,   20
Nor have I given a pension to my blood,
Or lavishly in play consumed your stock.
These, and the miseries that do attend them,
I dare with innocence proclaim are strangers
To all my temperate actions. For your daughter,   25
If there be any love to my deservings
Borne by her virtuous self, I cannot stop it;
Nor am I able to refrain her wishes.
She's private to herself and best of knowledge
Whom she'll make so happy as to sigh for.   30
Besides, I cannot think you mean to match her
Unto a fellow of so lame a presence,
One that hath little left of nature in him.

MERCHANT

'Tis very well, sir. I can tell your wisdom
How all this shall be cured.

JASPER   Your care becomes you.   35

MERCHANT

And thus it must be, sir: I here discharge you
My house and service. Take your liberty,
And when I want a son I'll send for you.   *Exit*

JASPER

These be the fair rewards of them that love.
Oh you that live in freedom, never prove   40
The travail of a mind led by desire!

Enter LUCE

LUCE

Why, how now, friend? Struck with my father's thunder?

13 *however* notwithstanding [my trust in you]
15 *factor* deputy (who buys and sells for his master)
28 *refrain* curb
29 *private . . . knowledge* free to decide and knows best
40 *prove* experience
41 *travail* suffering

JASPER
  Struck, and struck dead, unless the remedy
  Be full of speed and virtue. I am now
  What I expected long, no more your father's.   45
LUCE
  But mine.
JASPER   But yours, and only yours, I am;
  That's all I have to keep me from the statute.
  You dare be constant still?
LUCE   Oh, fear me not.
  In this I dare be better than a woman:
  Nor shall his anger nor his offers move me,   50
  Were they both equal to a prince's power.
JASPER
  You know my rival?
LUCE   Yes, and love him dearly,
  Even as I love an ague or foul weather;
  I prithee, Jasper, fear him not.
JASPER   Oh, no,
  I do not mean to do him so much kindness.   55
  But to our own desires: you know the plot
  We both agreed on?
LUCE   Yes, and will perform
  My part exactly.
JASPER   I desire no more
  Farewell, and keep my heart; 'tis yours.
LUCE   I take it;
  He must do miracles makes me forsake it.   *Exeunt*   60

CITIZEN
  Fie upon 'em, little infidels: what a matter's here now! Well,
  I'll be hanged for a halfpenny, if there be not some abomina-
  tion knavery in this play. Well, let 'em look to't. Rafe must
  come, and if there be any tricks a-brewing—
WIFE
  Let 'em brew and bake too, husband, a God's name. Rafe   65

---

44 *speed and virtue* goodness and power

47 *the statute.* Either that against 'Rogues, vagabonds, and sturdy beggars'
  (39 Eliz. Ch. 4) or 'the Statute of Apprentices' (5 Eliz. Ch. 4, ix–x),
  passed in 1562, which required all young persons to be apprenticed
  and any that departed from their master's parish without a testimonial
  to be imprisoned.

will find all out, I warrant you, and they were older than they are.—

[Enter BOY]

I pray, my pretty youth, is Rafe ready?

BOY

He will be presently.

WIFE

Now, I pray you, make my commendations unto him, and   70
withal carry him this stick of liquorice. Tell him his mistress
sent it him, and bid him bite a piece; 'twill open his pipes the
better, say.

[Exit BOY]

Enter MERCHANT *and* MASTER HUMPHREY

MERCHANT

Come, sir, she's yours; upon my faith, she's yours;
You have my hand. For other idle lets   75
Between your hopes and her, thus with a wind
They are scattered and no more. My wanton prentice,
That like a bladder blew himself with love,
I have let out, and sent him to discover
New masters yet unknown.

HUMPHREY   I thank you, sir,   80
Indeed, I thank you, sir; and ere I stir
It shall be known, however you do deem,
I am of gentle blood and gentle seem.

MERCHANT

Oh, sir, I know it certain.

HUMPHREY   Sir, my friend,
Although, as writers say, all things have end,   85
And that we call a pudding hath his two,
Oh, let it not seem strange, I pray, to you,
If in this bloody simile I put
My love, more endless than frail things or gut.

WIFE

Husband, I prithee, sweet lamb, tell me one thing, but tell   90

66 *and* if
75 *lets* obstacles
86 *pudding* blood sausage

72 *open his pipes.* Liquorice was used for loosening phlegm and clearing the voice (Murch); this is the first of a number of jibes at the Wife's trust in quack medicine.

me truly:—stay youths, I beseech you, till I question my
husband.

CITIZEN

What is it, mouse?

WIFE

Sirrah, didst thou ever see a prettier child? How it behaves
itself, I warrant ye, and speaks, and looks, and perts up the   95
head?—I pray you, brother, with your favour, were you
never none of Master Monkester's scholars?

CITIZEN

Chicken, I prithee heartily, contain thyself; the childer are
pretty childer; but when Rafe comes, lamb—

WIFE

Ay, when Rafe comes, cony.—Well, my youth, you may   100
proceed.

MERCHANT

Well, sir, you know my love, and rest, I hope,
Assured of my consent. Get but my daughter's,
And wed her when you please. You must be bold,
And clap in close unto her. Come, I know   105
You have language good enough to win a wench.

WIFE

A whoreson tyrant! H'as been an old stringer in's days, I
warrant him.

HUMPHREY

I take your gentle offer, and withal
Yield love again for love reciprocal.   110

MERCHANT

What, Luce! within there!

Enter LUCE

LUCE   Called you, sir?

MERCHANT   I did

Give entertainment to this gentleman

94 *prettier* cleverer, better trained
95 *perts* perks
107 *stringer* fornicator

---

97 *Monkester*. Richard Mulcaster was the Master of St Paul's school from
1596 to 1608; since the Children of Paul's had probably moved to the
rival Whitefriars Theatre in 1607–8 as the Children of the King's
Revels (see Harbage, p. 36), the Wife's remark is exceedingly tactless.

And see you be not froward.—To her, sir;
My presence will but be an eye-sore to you.   *Exit*

HUMPHREY
Fair Mistress Luce, how do you do? Are you well?   115
Give me your hand, and then I pray you tell
How doth you little sister and your brother,
And whether you love me or any other.

LUCE
Sir, these are quickly answered.

HUMPHREY   So they are,
Where women are not cruel. But how far   120
Is it now distant from this place we are in,
Unto that blessed place, your father's warren?

LUCE
What makes you think of that, sir?

HUMPHREY   Even that face;
For, stealing rabbits whilom in that place,
God Cupid, or the keeper, I know not whether,   125
Unto my cost and charges brought you thither,
And there began—

LUCE   Your game, sir.

HUMPHREY   Let no game,
Or any thing that tendeth to the same,
Be evermore remembered, thou fair killer,
For whom I sat me down and brake my tiller.   130

WIFE
There's a kind gentleman, I warrant you. When will you do
as much for me, George?

LUCE
Beshrew me, sir, I am sorry for your losses;
But as the proverb says, I cannot cry.
I would you had not seen me.

HUMPHREY   So would I,   135
Unless you had more maw to do me good.

LUCE
Why, cannot this strange passion be withstood?
Send for a constable and raise the town.

122 *warren* land for breeding game
125 *whether* which
130 *tiller* beam of crossbow, a sexual quibble
134 *proverb* 'I am sorry for thee but I cannot cry' (Tilley, C 872)
136 *maw* stomach, craving

HUMPHREY

 Oh no, my valiant love will batter down
 Millions of constables, and put to flight   140
 Even that great watch of Midsummer day at night.

LUCE

 Beshrew me, sir, 'twere good I yielded then;
 Weak women cannot hope, where valiant men
 Have no resistance.

HUMPHREY   Yield then; I am full

 Of pity, though I say it, and can pull   145
 Out of my pocket, thus, a pair of gloves.
 Look, Lucy, look: the dog's tooth nor the dove's
 Are not so white as these; and sweet they be,
 And whipped about with silk, as you may see.
 If you desire the price, shoot from your eye 150
 A beam to this place, and you shall espy
 F. S., which is to say, my sweetest honey,
 They cost me three and two pence, or no money.

LUCE

 Well, sir, I take them kindly, and I thank you.
 What would you more?

HUMPHREY   Nothing.

LUCE   Why then, farewell. 155

HUMPHREY

 Nor so, nor so; for, lady, I must tell,
 Before we part, for what we met together;
 God grant me time, and patience, and fair weather.

LUCE

 Speak, and declare your mind in terms so brief.

HUMPHREY

 I shall. Then, first and foremost, for relief 160
 I call to you, if that you can afford it;
 I care not at what price, for, on my word, it
 Shall be repaid again, although it cost me

---

150 *shoot* ed. sute Q1   161 *you, if* Q2 you, I if Q1

141 *that great watch.* An elaborate and popular pageant at which the City
 and companies mustered the militia and constables to serve for the
 ensuing year; see Stow, i. 101–3.
146 *gloves.* Were customarily presented as love-tokens at betrothals and
 weddings; see Brand, i. 277.
152 *F.S.* Probably a dealer's mark for the price (see R. Withington, ' "F.S.,
 which is to say . . ." ', *SP*, XXII [1925], pp. 226–33), or possibly
 Humphrey bought the gloves for someone else!
153 *three and two pence.* The gloves were expensive.

More than I'll speak of now. For love hath tossed me
In furious blanket like a tennis-ball,   165
And now I rise aloft, and now I fall.

LUCE
Alas, good gentleman, alas the day.

HUMPHREY
I thank you heartily, and, as I say,
Thus do I still continue without rest,
I'th' morning like a man, at night a beast,   170
Roaring and bellowing mine own disquiet,
That much I fear, forsaking of my diet
Will bring me presently to that quandàry,
I shall bid all adieu.

LUCE   Now, by Saint Mary,
That were great pity.

HUMPHREY   So it were, beshrew me.   175
Then ease me, lusty Luce, and pity show me.

LUCE
Why, sir, you know my will is nothing worth
Without my father's grant; get his consent,
And then you may with assurance try me.

HUMPHREY
The worshipful your sire will not deny me;   180
For I have asked him, and he hath replied,
'Sweet Master Humphrey, Luce shall be thy bride'.

LUCE
Sweet Master Humphrey, then I am content.

HUMPHREY
And so am I, in truth.

LUCE   Yet take me with you;
There is another clause must be annexed,   185
And this it is: I swore and will perform it,
No man shall ever joy me as his wife
But he that stole me hence. If you dare venture,
I am yours—you need not fear, my father loves you—
If not, farewell for ever.

HUMPHREY   Stay, nymph, stay;   190
I have a double gelding, coloured bay,

173 *quandary* original stressing was quandàry
176 *lusty* pretty
184 *take me with you* let this be clear
191 *double gelding* horse for two

172 *diet.* Imposed as a cure for venereal disease.

 Sprung by his father from Barbarian kind;
 Another for myself, though somewhat blind,
 Yet true as trusty tree.
LUCE   I am satisfied;
 And so I give my hand. Our course must lie   195
 Through Waltham Forest, where I have a friend
 Will entertain us. So, farewell, Sir Humphrey,
 And think upon your business.   *Exit* LUCE
HUMPHREY   Though I die,
 I am resolved to venture life and limb
 For one so young, so fair, so kind, so trim.   200
           Exit HUMPHREY

WIFE
 By my faith and troth, George, and, as I am virtuous, it is
 e'en the kindest young man that ever trod on shoe leather.
 Well, go thy ways; if thou hast her not, 'tis not thy fault,
 'faith.
CITIZEN
 I prithee, mouse, be patient; 'a shall have her, or I'll make   205
 some of 'em smoke for't.
WIFE
 That's my good lamb, George. Fie, this stinking tobacco
 kills me; would there were none in England.—Now I pray,
 gentlemen, what good does this stinking tobacco do you?
 Nothing, I warrant you; make chimneys o'your faces.—Oh,   210
 husband, husband, now, now, there's Rafe, there's Rafe.

  Enter RAFE *like a grocer in's shop, with two*
 prentices [TIM *and* GEORGE] *reading* Palmerin of England

206 *of* Q2 (om. Q1)   206 *smoke* suffer
208 *me* ed. men Q1–3, F

---

192 *Barbarian.* From the Saracen countries of North Africa (<Berber),
 famous for their breeds of horses.
196 *Waltham Forest.* Waltham Cross is in Hertfordshire, 12 miles N. of
 London; part of the great forest survives at Epping.
207 *tobacco.* After Sir Walter Ralegh had made smoking fashionable
 among gallants, the habit provoked many attacks including *The Meta-*
 morphosis of Tobacco (1602), a poem by the dramatist's brother John, and
 James I's *A Counterblaste to Tobacco* (1604).
211 s.d. *like a grocer in's shop.* Rafe is wearing the blue of a serving-man,
 not the livery ordered by the Citizen.
211 s.d. *Palmerin of England.* In fact Rafe reads out of *Palmerin d'Oliva*, I.
 li, to which *Palmerin of England* was a sequel; both had been translated
 into English by Antony Munday.

CITIZEN

Peace, fool, let Rafe alone.—Hark you, Rafe; do not strain
yourself too much at the first.—Peace!—Begin, Rafe.

RAFE [*reads*]

'Then Palmerin and Trineus, snatching their lances from
their dwarfs, and clasping their helmets, galloped amain after   215
the giant; and Palmerin, having gotten a sight of him, came
posting amain, saying: "Stay, traitorous thief, for thou mayst
not so carry away her that is worth the greatest lord in the
world"; and with these words gave him a blow on the shoul-
der, that he struck him besides his elephant; and Trineus,   220
coming to the knight that had Agricola behind him, set him
soon besides his horse, with his neck broken in the fall, so
that the princess, getting out of the throng, between joy and
grief said: "All happy knight, the mirror of all such as follow
arms, now may I be well assured of the love thou bearest   225
me".' I wonder why the kings do not raise an army of fourteen
or fifteen hundred thousand men, as big as the army that the
Prince of Portigo brought against Rosicleer, and destroy
these giants; they do much hurt to wandering damsels that
go in quest of their knights.   230

WIFE

Faith, husband, and Rafe says true; for they say the King of
Portugal cannot sit at his meat, but the giants and the ettins
will come and snatch it from him.

CITIZEN

Hold thy tongue.—On, Rafe.

RAFE

And certainly those knights are much to be commended, who   235
neglecting their possessions, wander with a squire and a
dwarf through the deserts to relieve poor ladies.

221–2 *set . . . horse* unhorsed him   228 *Portigo* Portugal
224 *mirror* paragon   232 *ettins* giants from Germanic folklore

---

220 *elephant*. The original has 'horse', but the exaggeration is intentional.
221 *Agricola*. The princess Palmerin is rescuing. In the Spanish text and Munday's
     translation the name is 'Agriola'. Perhaps the perversion 'Agricola' is a joke: see
     Richard Proudfoot, 'Francis Beaumont and the Hidden Princess', *The Library*,
     IV (1982), pp. 47–9.
228 *Rosicleer*. Hero of Ortuñez de Calahorra's *Espejo de Principes y Caual-
     leros*, one of the romances owned by Don Quixote, translated into
     English by Margaret Tyler and others as *The Mirror of Knighthood*
     (1578–1601).

WIFE

Ay, by my faith, are they, Rafe; let 'em say what they will,
they are indeed. Our knights neglect their possessions well
enough, but they do not the rest.   240

RAFE

There are no such courteous and fair well-spoken knights in
this age: they will call one 'the son of a whore', that Palmerin
of England would have called 'fair sir'; and one that Rosicleer would have called 'right beauteous damsel', they will
call 'damned bitch'.   245

WIFE

I'll be sworn will they, Rafe; they have called me so an hun-
red times about a scurvy pipe of tobacco.

RAFE

But what brave spirit could be content to sit in his shop with
a flappet of wood and a blue apron before him, selling mithridatum and dragon's water to visited houses, that might   250
pursue feats of arms, and through his noble achievements
procure such a famous history to be written of his heroic
prowess?

CITIZEN

Well said, Rafe, some more of those words, Rafe.

WIFE

They go finely, by my troth.   255

RAFE

Why should not I then pursue this course, both for the credit
of myself and our company? For amongst all the worthy
books of achievements I do not call to mind that I yet read
of a grocer errant. I will be the said knight. Have you heard
of any that hath wandered unfurnished of his squire and   260
dwarf? My elder prentice Tim shall be my trusty squire, and

249 *flappet* small flap (of the counter or the shop's shutter)
249–50 *mithridatum* herbal medicine named after King Mithridates,
  used against poison and disease
250 *dragon's water* used against fevers and the plague
250 *visited* by plague

---

240 *do not the rest.* Possibly an allusion to the sale of knighthoods by James I.
258 For specific similarities between Rafe's adventures and the romances
  see Murch's notes *passim*.

little George my dwarf. Hence my blue apron! Yet in remem-
brance of my former trade, upon my shield shall be portrayed
a burning pestle, and I will be called the Knight o'th' Burn-
ing Pestle.   265

WIFE

Nay, I dare swear thou wilt not forget thy old trade; thou
wert ever meek.

RAFE

Tim.

TIM

Anon.

RAFE

My beloved squire, and George my dwarf, I charge you that   270
from henceforth you never call me by any other name but
the 'Right Courteous and Valiant Knight of the Burning
Pestle', and that you never call any female by the name of a
woman or wench, but 'Fair Lady', if she have her desires, if
not, 'Distressed Damsel'; that you call all forests and heaths   275
'deserts', and all horses 'palfreys'.

WIFE

This is very fine, faith. Do the gentlemen like Rafe, think
you, husband?

CITIZEN

Ay, I warrant thee, the players would give all the shoes in
their shop for him.   280

RAFE

My beloved squire Tim, stand out. Admit this were a desert,
and over it a knight errant pricking, and I should bid you
inquire of his intents, what would you say?

TIM

Sir, my master sent me to know whither you are riding?

RAFE

No, thus: 'Fair sir, the Right Courteous and Valiant Knight   285

282 *pricking* spurring, riding (see *The Faerie Queene*, I.i, 1)
284 *you* Q2 your Q1

279–80 *shoes in their shop*. Actors' costumes at this time were elaborate
      and costly.
282 *pricking*. Chaucer too rang the changes on this word throughout his
      parody *Sir Thopas*.

of the Burning Pestle commanded me to inquire upon what
adventure you are bound, whether to relieve some distressed
damsels, or otherwise'.

CITIZEN
Whoreson blockhead cannot remember!
WIFE
I'faith, and Rafe told him on't before; all the gentlemen   290
heard him.—Did he not, gentlemen? did not Rafe tell him
on't?

GEORGE
Right Courteous and Valiant Knight of the Burning Pestle,
here is a distressed damsel, to have a halfpenny-worth of
pepper.   295

WIFE
That's a good boy. See, the little boy can hit it; by my troth,
it's a fine child.

RAFE
Relieve her with all courteous language. Now shut up shop;
no more my prentice, but my trusty squire and dwarf. I must
bespeak my shield and arming pestle.   300
                          [*Exeunt* TIM *and* GEORGE]

CITIZEN
Go thy ways, Rafe. As I'm a true man, thou art the best on
'em all.
WIFE
Rafe, Rafe.
RAFE
What say you, mistress?
WIFE
I prithee come again quickly, sweet Rafe.   305
RAFE
By and by.   *Exit* RAFE

Enter JASPER *and his mother*, MISTRESS MERRYTHOUGHT

MISTRESS MERRYTHOUGHT
Give thee my blessing? No, I'll ne'er give thee my blessing;
I'll see thee hanged first; it shall ne'er be said I gave thee

287 *you* Q2 your Q1   300 *arming* armorial

my blessing. Th'art thy father's own son, of the right blood
of the Merrythoughts. I may curse the time that e'er I knew   310
thy father; he hath spent all his own, and mine too, and
when I tell him of it, he laughs and dances, and sings, and
cries, 'A merry heart lives long-a'. And thou art a wastethrift, and art run away from thy master that loved thee
well, and art come to me; and I have laid up a little for my   315
younger son Michael, and thou think'st to bezzle that, but
thou shalt never be able to do it.

Enter MICHAEL

—Come hither, Michael, come, Michael, down on thy
knees; thou shalt have my blessing.
MICHAEL
    I pray you, mother, pray to God to bless me.   320
MISTRESS MERRYTHOUGHT
    God bless thee; but Jasper shall never have my blessing. He
    shall be hanged first, shall he not, Michael? How say'st thou?
MICHAEL
    Yes, forsooth, mother, and grace of God.
MISTRESS MERRYTHOUGHT
    That's a good boy.

WIFE
    I'faith, it's a fine spoken child.   325

JASPER
    Mother, though you forget a parent's love,
    I must preserve the duty of a child.
    I ran not from my master, nor return
    To have your stock maintain my idleness.

WIFE
    Ungracious child, I warrant him; hark how he chops logic   330
    with his mother!—Thou hadst best tell her she lies; do, tell
    her she lies.

313–14 *wastethrift* spendthrift
316 *bezzle* squander
330 *chops logic* bandies arguments

313 '*A merry heart lives long-a*'. A line from the song sung by Autolycus
    in *The Winter's Tale*, IV. iii, and by Silence in *2 Henry IV*, V. iii.

CITIZEN
   If he were my son, I would hang him up by the heels, and
   flay him, and salt him, whoreson halter-sack!

JASPER
   My coming only is to beg your love,   335
   Which I must ever, though I never gain it.
   And howsoever you esteem of me,
   There is no drop of blood hid in these veins
   But I remember well belongs to you
   That brought me forth, and would be glad for you   340
   To rip them all again, and let it out.
MISTRESS MERRYTHOUGHT
   I'faith, I had sorrow enough for thee, God knows; but I'll
   hamper thee well enough. Get thee in, thou vagabond, get
   thee in, and learn of thy brother Michael.
                              [*Exeunt* JASPER *and* MICHAEL]
OLD MERRYTHOUGHT ([*sings*] *within*)
             Nose, nose, jolly red nose,   345
             And who gave thee this jolly red nose?
MISTRESS MERRYTHOUGHT
   Hark, my husband; he's singing and hoiting, and I'm fain to
   cark and care, and all little enough.—Husband, Charles,
   Charles Merrythought.

                    Enter OLD MERRYTHOUGHT

OLD MERRYTHOUGHT [*sings*]
             Nutmegs and ginger, cinnamon and cloves,   350
             And they gave me this jolly red nose.
MISTRESS MERRYTHOUGHT
   If you would consider your state, you would have little list
   to sing, iwis.
OLD MERRYTHOUGHT
   It should never be considered while it were an estate, if I
   thought it would spoil my singing.   355

334 *halter-sack* gallows-bird
347 *hoiting* roistering
348 *cark* fret
352 *state* estate, dignity
352 *list* desire
353 *iwis* for certain

345–51 *Nose . . . nose*. The refrain to a song from Thomas Ravenscroft's
    Deuteromelia (1609), no. 7; reprinted in Chappell, i. 141–2.

MISTRESS MERRYTHOUGHT

But how wilt thou do, Charles? Thou art an old man, and
thou canst not work, and thou hast not forty shillings left,
and thou eatest good meat, and drinkest good drink, and
laughest?

OLD MERRYTHOUGHT

And will do.   360

MISTRESS MERRYTHOUGHT

But how wilt thou come by it, Charles?

OLD MERRYTHOUGHT

How? Why, how have I done hitherto this forty years? I
never came into my dining room, but at eleven and six o'clock
I found excellent meat and drink o'th'table; my clothes were
never worn out, but next morning a tailor brought me a new   365
suit; and without question it will be so ever. Use makes
perfectness. If all should fail, it is but a little straining myself
extraordinary, and laugh myself to death.

WIFE

It's a foolish old man this: is not he, George?

CITIZEN

Yes, cony.   370

WIFE

Give me a penny i'th'purse while I live, George.

CITIZEN

Ay, by lady, cony, hold thee there.

MISTRESS MERRYTHOUGHT

Well, Charles, you promised to provide for Jasper, and I
have laid up for Michael. I pray you, pay Jasper his portion;
he's come home, and he shall not consume Michael's stock.   375
He says his master turned him away, but I promise you
truly, I think he ran away.

WIFE

No, indeed, Mistress Merrythought, though he be a notable
gallows, yet I'll assure you his master did turn him away,

366–7 *Use makes perfectness* (Tilley, U 24)
372 *hold thee there* stick to that
374 *portion* share of property given to an heir
378–9 *notable gallows* notorious gallows-bird

363 *eleven .. . . o'clock.* The hours of the two main meals.

even in this place; 'twas, i'faith, within this half hour, about   380
his daughter; my husband was by.

CITIZEN
Hang him, rogue. He served him well enough: love his
master's daughter! By my troth, cony, if there were a thousand
boys, thou wouldst spoil them all with taking their parts.
Let his mother alone with him.   385

WIFE
Ay, George, but yet truth is truth.

OLD MERRYTHOUGHT
Where is Jasper? He's welcome how ever. Call him in; he
shall have his portion. Is he merry?

MISTRESS MERRYTHOUGHT
Ay, foul chive him, he is too merry.—Jasper! Michael!

Enter JASPER *and* MICHAEL

OLD MERRYTHOUGHT
Welcome, Jasper, though thou run'st away, welcome; God   390
bless thee. 'Tis thy mother's mind thou shouldst receive thy
portion; thou hast been abroad, and I hope hast learned experience enough to govern it; thou art of sufficient years.
Hold thy hand: one, two, three, four, five, six, seven, eight,
nine, there's ten shillings for thee. Thrust thyself into the   395
world with that, and take some settled course. If fortune
cross thee, thou hast a retiring place; come home to me; I
have twenty shillings left. Be a good husband, that is, wear
ordinary clothes, eat the best meat, and drink the best drink;
be merry, and give to the poor, and believe me, thou hast no   400
end of thy goods.

JASPER
Long may you live free from all thought of ill,
And long have cause to be thus merry still.
But, father—

OLD MERRYTHOUGHT
No more words, Jasper, get thee gone; thou hast my blessing;   405
thy father's spirit upon thee. Farewell, Jasper. [*sings*]

---

384 *parts* pun on roles and sexual organs
387 *how ever* in any case
389 *foul chive* ill betide
389 s.d. *Enter . . .* MICHAEL Q1 prints below line 388
397 *cross* thwart
398 *Be . . . husband* be thrifty and prudent

> *But yet, or ere you part, oh cruel,*
> *Kiss me, kiss me, sweeting, mine own dear jewel.*

So, now begone; no words.   *Exit* JASPER

MISTRESS MERRYTHOUGHT

So, Michael, now get thee gone too.   410

MICHAEL

Yes forsooth, mother; but I'll have my father's blessing first.

MISTRESS MERRYTHOUGHT

No, Michael, 'tis no matter for his blessing; thou hast my
blessing; begone. I'll fetch my money and jewels and follow
thee; I'll stay no longer with him, I warrant thee.

                                        Exit MICHAEL

—Truly, Charles, I'll begone too.   415

OLD MERRYTHOUGHT

What! you will not?

MISTRESS MERRYTHOUGHT

Yes, indeed will I.

OLD MERRYTHOUGHT [*sings*]

> *Hey-ho, farewell, Nan,*
> *I'll never trust wench more again, if I can.*

MISTRESS MERRYTHOUGHT

You shall not think, when all your own is gone, to spend that   420
I have been scraping up for Michael.

OLD MERRYTHOUGHT

Farewell, good wife, I expect it not; all I have to do in this
world is to be merry; which I shall, if the ground be not taken
from me; and if it be, [*sings*]

> *When earth and seas from me are reft,*   425
> *The skies aloft for me are left.*

                                        Exeunt

Finis Actus primi

---

412 *no matter* Q2 now matter Q1
425 *reft* p.p. of 'reave', take away

407–8 *But yet . . . jewel.* From a song (no. xv) in John Dowland's *The First
Booke of Songes or Ayres* (1597), transcribed in E. H. Fellowes, *The
English School of Lutenist Song Writers* (London, 1921), First Series,
ii. 60–1.

[Interlude I]

Boy danceth. Music.

WIFE
I'll be sworn he's a merry old gentleman for all that. Hark,
hark, husband, hark! fiddles, fiddles! Now surely they go
finely. They say 'tis present death for these fiddlers to tune
their rebecks before the great Turk's grace, is't not, George?
But look, look, here's a youth dances.—Now, good youth, do   5
a turn o'th' toe.—Sweetheart, i'faith, I'll have Rafe come and
do some of his gambols.—He'll ride the wild mare, gentlemen, 'twould do your hearts good to see him.—I thank you,
kind youth; pray, bid Rafe come.

CITIZEN
Peace, cony.—Sirrah, you scurvy boy, bid the players send   10
Rafe, or by God's — and they do not, I'll tear some of their
periwigs beside their heads: this is all riff-raff.

[Act II]

Enter MERCHANT *and* HUMPHREY

MERCHANT
And how, faith, how goes it now, son Humphrey?

HUMPHREY
Right worshipful, and my beloved friend
And father dear, this matter's at an end.

3 *present* immediate
4 *rebecks* early form of fiddle with three strings
7 *wild mare* see-saw, hence be lively
Act II ed. Actus secundi Scœna prima Q1

Int. s.d. Dancing and music were customary in the interludes between the
acts of a play.
  3–4 *They say . . . Turk's grace.* Sultans were proverbially fearsome des-
  pots; Fynes Moryson, who had been in Turkey in 1595, wrote in the
  Fourth Part of his *Itinerary* (written in 1617–20, but unpublished
  until 1903) of the Emperor Amurath (1574–95); 'He loued Musick,
  but had not the patience to attend the tuning of instruments', *Itinerary*,
  ed. C. Hughes (London, 1903), I. i, 4.
  11 The word omitted is probably 'body'—the 'Act to Restrain the Abuses
  of the Players' (3 James Ch.21) of 1606 had sought to quell profanity;
  but cf. II, 229 where Humphrey swears by the sacrament, the sign of
  a swell.
  12 *periwigs*. Were frequently worn by actors at this time, cf. *Hamlet*, III.
  ii, 12.

MERCHANT
  'Tis well; it should be so; I'm glad the girl
  Is found so tractable.
HUMPHREY   Nay, she must whirl   5
  From hence (and you must wink; for so, I say,
  The story tells) tomorrow before day.

WIFE
  George, dost thou think in thy conscience now 'twill be a
  match? Tell me but what thou think'st, sweet rogue. Thou
  seest the poor gentleman, dear heart, how it labours and   10
  throbs, I warrant you, to be at rest. I'll go move the father
  for't.
CITIZEN
  No, no, I prithee sit still, honeysuckle; thou'lt spoil all. If he
  deny him, I'll bring half a dozen good fellows myself, and in
  the shutting of an evening knock't up, and there's an end.   15
WIFE
  I'll buss thee for that, i'faith, boy. Well, George, well, you
  have been a wag in your days, I warrant you; but God forgive
  you, and I do with all my heart.

MERCHANT
  How was it, son? You told me that tomorrow
  Before day break you must convey her hence?   20
HUMPHREY
  I must, I must, and thus it is agreed:
  Your daughter rides upon a brown-bay steed,
  I on a sorrel, which I bought of Brian,
  The honest host of the Red Roaring Lion,
  In Waltham situate. Then, if you may,   25
  Consent in seemly sort, lest by delay
  The fatal sisters come and do the office,
  And then you'll sing another song.
MERCHANT   Alas,
  Why should you be thus full of grief to me,
  That do willing as yourself agree   30
  To anything, so it be good and fair?

  6 *wink* turn a blind eye
  15 *shutting of an evening* close of day, i.e. a short time
  15 *knock't up* put an end to the business
  16 *buss* kiss
  23 *sorrel* chestnut horse

Then steal her when you will, if such a pleasure
Content you both; I'll sleep and never see it,
To make your joys more full. But tell me why
You may not here perform your marriage?   35

WIFE
God's blessing o'thy soul, old man! I'faith, thou art loath to
part true hearts, I see.—'A has her, George, and I'm as glad
on't.—Well, go thy ways, Humphrey, for a fair-spoken man;
I believe thou hast not thy fellow within the walls of London;
and I should say the suburbs too I should not lie.—Why   40
dost not rejoice with me, George?

CITIZEN
If I could but see Rafe again, I were as merry as mine host,
i'faith.

HUMPHREY
The cause you seem to ask, I thus declare
(Help me, oh Muses nine): your daughter sware   45
A foolish oath, the more it was the pity;
Yet none but myself within this city
Shall dare to say so, but a bold defiance
Shall meet him, were he of the noble science.
And yet she sware, and yet why did she swear?   50
Truly, I cannot tell, unless it were
For her own ease, for sure sometimes an oath,
Being sworn, thereafter is like cordial broth.
And this it was she swore: never to marry
But such a one whose mighty arm could carry   55
(As meaning me, for I am such a one)
Her bodily away through stick and stone,
Till both of us arrive, at her request,
Some ten miles off, in the wild Waltham Forest.

MERCHANT
If this be all, you shall not need to fear   60
Any denial in your love. Proceed;
I'll neither follow nor repent the deed.

---

49 *science* of defence, i.e. boxing or fencing
53 *cordial* restorative

---

40 *suburbs*. For a description of these unsavoury areas just outside the
walls where the citizens resorted for pleasure see Stow, ii. 69–97.

HUMPHREY

Good night, twenty good nights, and twenty more.
And twenty more good nights—that makes threescore.

Exeunt

Enter MISTRESS MERRYTHOUGHT [*with jewel
casket and purse of money*], *and her son* MICHAEL

MISTRESS MERRYTHOUGHT

Come, Michael, art thou not weary, boy?   65

MICHAEL

No, forsooth, mother, not I.

MISTRESS MERRYTHOUGHT

Where be we now, child?

MICHAEL

Indeed, forsooth, mother, I cannot tell, unless we be at Mile
End. Is not all the world Mile End, mother?

MISTRESS MERRYTHOUGHT

No, Michael, not all the world, boy; but I can assure thee,   70
Michael, Mile End is a goodly matter; there has been a
pitch-field, my child, between the naughty Spaniels and the
English men; and the Spaniels ran away, Michael, and the
English men followed. My neighbour Coxstone was there,
boy, and killed them all with a birding piece.   75

MICHAEL

Mother, forsooth—

MISTRESS MERRYTHOUGHT

What says my white boy?

MICHAEL

Shall not my father go with us too?

72 *pitch-field* regular battle
72 *naughty* wicked
72 *Spaniels* she means Spaniards
77 *white* darling

63–4 For possible parodies in these lines see Baldwin Maxwell, ' "Twenty
Good Nights"—*The Knight of the Burning Pestle* and Middleton's
Family of Love', *MLN*, LXIII (1948), pp. 233–7; and W. J. Olive,
' "Twenty Good Nights"—*The Knight of the Burning Pestle*, *The
Family of Love*, and *Romeo and Juliet*', *SP*, XLVII (1950), pp. 182–9.
68 *Mile End*. A hamlet one mile from Aldgate used as a training-ground
for the citizen forces. Entertainments were also held there, including
mock-battles like the one described in the Fiddler's ballad in *Monsieur
Thomas*, III. iii: 'The Landing of the Spaniards at Bow, with the
Bloody Battle at Mile-End'. This is probably the incident to which
Mistress Merrythought refers.

MISTRESS MERRYTHOUGHT
No, Michael, let thy father go snick up; he shall never come
between a pair of sheets with me again while he lives. Let   80
him stay at home and sing for his supper, boy. Come, child,
sit down, and I'll show my boy fine knacks indeed. Look
here, Michael, here's a ring, and here's a brooch, and here's
a bracelet, and here's two rings more, and here's money and
gold by th'eye, my boy.   85
MICHAEL
Shall I have all this, mother?
MISTRESS MERRYTHOUGHT
Ay, Michael, thou shalt have all, Michael.

CITIZEN
How lik'st thou this, wench?
WIFE
I cannot tell; I would have Rafe, George; I'll see no more
else, indeed la, and I pray you let the youths understand so   90
much by word of mouth; for I tell you truly, I'm afraid o'
my boy. Come, come, George, let's be merry and wise. The
child's a fatherless child; and say they should put him into
a strait pair of gaskins, 'twere worse than knot-grass: he
would never grow after it.   95

Enter RAFE, [TIM *as*] *Squire, and* [GEORGE *as*] *Dwarf*

CITIZEN
Here's Rafe, here's Rafe.
WIFE
How do you, Rafe? You are welcome, Rafe, as I may say;
it's a good boy, hold up thy head, and be not afraid; we are
thy friends, Rafe; the gentlemen will praise thee, Rafe, if
thou play'st thy part with audacity. Begin, Rafe, o'God's   100
name.

RAFE
My trusty squire, unlace my helm; give me my hat. Where
are we, or what desert may this be?

79 *snick up* hang himself   82 *knacks* trinkets
85 *by th'eye* in unlimited quantities
90 *youths* boy actors
94 *strait* tight
94 *gaskins* breeches
94 *knot-grass* supposed to stunt growth; cf. *A Midsummer Night's
Dream*, III. ii, 329

GEORGE

    Mirror of knighthood, this is, as I take it, the perilous
    Waltham Down, in whose bottom stands the enchanted   105
    valley.

MISTRESS MERRYTHOUGHT

    Oh Michael, we are betrayed, we are betrayed! Here be
    giants! Fly, boy; fly, boy; fly!

    Exeunt MOTHER *and* MICHAEL [*dropping purse and casket*]

RAFE

    Lace on my helm again. What noise is this?
    A gentle lady flying the embrace   110
    Of some uncourteous knight? I will relieve her.
    Go, squire, and say, the knight that wears this pestle
    In honour of all ladies, swears revenge
    Upon that recreant coward that pursues her.
    Go comfort her, and that same gentle squire   115
    That bears her company.

TIM   I go, brave knight.

                                [*Exit*]

RAFE

    My trusty dwarf and friend, reach me my shield,
    And hold it while I swear. First by my knighthood;
    Then by the soul of Amadis de Gaul,
    My famous ancestor; then by my sword   120
    The beauteous Brionella girt about me;
    By this bright burning pestle, of mine honour
    The living trophy; and by all respect
    Due to distressed damsels: here I vow
    Never to end the quest of this fair lady   125
    And that forsaken squire, till by my valour
    I gain their liberty.

GEORGE   Heaven bless the knight

    That thus relieves poor errant gentlewomen.   *Exeunt*

104 Henceforward Q1 substitutes the speech prefix DWARFE for
    GEORGE
114 *recreant* cowardly, false
116 Henceforward Q1 substitutes the speech prefix SQUIRE for TIM
128 s.d. *Exeunt* ed. *Exit* Q1.

---

104 See note to I, 228.
119 *Amadis de Gaul.* Hero of the Iberian romance of that name (1508);
    the English translation by Antony Munday appeared in parts 1590–
    1618.
121 *Brionella.* The mistress of Palmerin's (see I, 211n.) friend Ptolome
    (Murch).

WIFE

    Ay, marry, Rafe, this has some savour in't.—I would see the
proudest of them all offer to carry his books after him. But,   130
George, I will not have him go away so soon; I shall be sick
if he go away, that I shall. Call Rafe again, George, call Rafe
again; I prithee, sweetheart, let him come fight before me,
and let's ha' some drums and some trumpets, and let him
kill all that comes near him, and thou lov'st me, George.   135

CITIZEN

    Peace a little, bird; he shall kill them all, and they were twenty
more on 'em than there are.

Enter JASPER

JASPER

    Now, Fortune, if thou be'st not only ill,
Show me thy better face, and bring about
Thy desperate wheel, that I may climb at length   140
And stand. This is our place of meeting,
If love have any constancy. Oh age,
Where only wealthy men are counted happy!
How shall I please thee, how deserve thy smiles,
When I am only rich in misery?   145
My father's blessing, and this little coin
Is my inheritance, a strong revénue!
From earth thou art, and to earth I give thee.
                [*Casts the money away*]
There grow and multiply, whilst fresher air
Breeds me a fresher fortune.—How, illusion?   150
                  Spies the casket
What, hath the devil coined himself before me?
'Tis metal good, it rings well; I am walking,
And taking too, I hope. Now God's dear blessing
Upon his heart that left it here. 'Tis mine;
These pearls, I take it, were not left for swine.   155
                      Exit

WIFE

    I do not like that this unthrifty youth should embezzle away

---

130 *carry his books* follow like a lowly pedant; cf. Tilley, B 533
151 *coined* formed   156 *embezzle* squander

---

140 *Thy desperate wheel.* The goddess Fortuna was customarily shown
    turning a wheel, signifying the short life of man's felicity.
148 A parody of parable of talents where one of the servants buried his
    lord's money in the ground, Matthew xxv. 14 ff.

the money; the poor gentlewoman his mother will have a
heavy heart for it, God knows.

CITIZEN

And reason good, sweetheart.

WIFE

But let him go. I'll tell Rafe a tale in's ear shall fetch him   160
again with a wanion, I warrant him, if he be above ground;
and besides, George, here are a number of sufficient gentlemen can witness, and myself, and yourself, and the musicians,
if we be called in question. But here comes Rafe, George;
thou shalt hear him speak, an he were an emperal.   165

Enter RAFE *and* [GEORGE *as*] *Dwarf*

RAFE

Comes not Sir Squire again?

GEORGE   Right courteous knight,
Your squire doth come and with him comes the lady,

Enter MISTRESS MERRYTHOUGHT *and* MICHAEL,
and [TIM *as*] *Squire*

For and the Squire of Damsels, as I take it.

RAFE

Madam, if any service or devoir
Of a poor errant knight may right your wrongs,   170
Command it; I am prest to give you succour,
For to the holy end I bear my armour.

MISTRESS MERRYTHOUGHT

Alas, sir, I am a poor gentlewoman, and I have lost my
money in this forest.

161 *wanion* vengeance
162 *sufficient* able
165 *an* as if
165 *emperal* solecism for emperor
168 *For and* as well as
169 *devoir* duty
171 *prest* prepared (French *prêt*)

---

167 With this episode compare *Palmerin d'Oliva*, I. xxi: 'Howe *Palmerin* and
Ptolome met with a Damosell, who made great mone for a Casket which
two Knights had forcibly taken from her, and what happened to them',
tr. A. Munday (London, 1588).

168 *the Squire of Damsels.* In Spenser's *The Faerie Queene*, III. vii, 51 ff.,
appears the Squire of Dames whose task it is to find three hundred
ladies who would 'abide for euer chaste and sound'. When Satyrane
meets him he has found three.

RAFE

    Desert, you would say, lady, and not lost   175
    Whilst I have sword and lance. Dry up your tears,
    Which ill befit the beauty of that face,
    And tell the story, if I may request it,
    Of your disastrous fortune.

MISTRESS MERRYTHOUGHT

    Out, alas! I left a thousand pound, a thousand pound, e'en   180
    all the money I had laid up for this youth, upon the sight of
    your mastership; you looked so grim, and, as I may say it,
    saving your presence, more like a giant than a mortal man.

RAFE

    I am as you are, lady; so are they
    All mortal. But why weeps this gentle squire?   185

MISTRESS MERRYTHOUGHT

    Has he not cause to weep, do you think, when he hath lost
    his inheritance?

RAFE

    Young hope of valour, weep not; I am here
    That will confound thy foe and pay it dear
    Upon his coward head, that dares deny   190
    Distressed squires and ladies equity.
    I have but one horse, on which shall ride
    This lady fair behind me, and before
    This courteous squire; fortune will give us more
    Upon our next adventure. Fairly speed   195
    Beside us, squire and dwarf, to do us need.   *Exeunt*

CITIZEN

    Did not I tell you, Nell, what your man would do? By the
    faith of my body, wench, for clean action and good delivery
    they may all cast their caps at him.

WIFE

    And so they may, i'faith, for I dare speak it boldly, the   200
    twelve companies of London cannot match him, timber for

177 *befit* ed. befits Q1   185 *All* wholly
191 *equity* justice
199 *cast their caps at him* despair of imitating (Tilley, C 62)
201–2 *timber for timber* like for like

200–2 *the twelve companies.* These were the Mercers, the Grocers, the Drapers,
    the Fishmongers, the Goldsmiths, the Skinners, the Merchant Tailors,
    the Haberdashers, the Salters, the Ironmongers, the Vintners, and the
    Clothworkers; see W. C. Hazlitt, *The Livery Companies of the City of
    London* (London, 1892).

timber. Well, George, and he be not inveigled by some of
these paltry players, I ha' much marvel; but, George, we ha'
done our parts if the boy have any grace to be thankful.

CITIZEN

Yes, I warrant thee, duckling.   205

Enter HUMPHREY *and* LUCE

HUMPHREY

Good Mistress Luce, however I in fault am
For your lame horse, you're welcome unto Waltham.
But which way now to go or what to say
I know not truly till it be broad day.

LUCE

Oh fear not, Master Humphrey, I am guide   210
For this place good enough.

HUMPHREY   Then up and ride,
Or, if it please you, walk for your repose,
Or sit, or if you will, go pluck a rose;
Either of which shall be indifferent
To your good friend and Humphrey, whose consent   215
Is so entangled ever to your will,
As the poor harmless horse is to the mill.

LUCE

Faith, and you say the word, we'll e'en sit down
And take a nap.

HUMPHREY   'Tis better in the town,
Where we may nap together; for, believe me,   220
To sleep without a snatch would mickle grieve me.

LUCE

You're merry, Master Humphrey.

HUMPHREY   So I am,
And have been ever merry from my dam.

LUCE

Your nurse had the less labour.

HUMPHREY   Faith, it may be,
Unless it were by chance I did beray me.   225

213 *go pluck a rose* make water (Tilley, R 184)
220 *nap* pun meaning both sleep and drink
221 *snatch* snack
225 *beray me* befoul myself

---

202 *inveigled.* Masters of the boy troupes on occasion kidnapped likely
    actors; see Harbage, p. 40.

Enter JASPER

JASPER
  Luce, dear friend Luce!
LUCE   Here, Jasper.
JASPER   You are mine.
HUMPHREY
  If it be so, my friend, you use me fine;
  What do you think I am?
JASPER   An arrant noddy.
HUMPHREY
  A word of obloquy! Now, by God's body,
  I'll tell thy master, for I know thee well.   230
JASPER
  Nay, and you be so forward for to tell,
  Take that, and that, and tell him, sir, I gave it, [*Beats him*]
  And say I paid you well.
HUMPHREY   Oh, sir, I have it,
  And do confess the payment. Pray be quiet.
JASPER
  Go, get to your night-cap and the diet   235
  To cure your beaten bones.
LUCE   Alas, poor Humphrey,
  Get thee some wholesome broth with sage and comfrey;
  A little oil of roses and a feather
  To 'noint thy back withal.
HUMPHREY   When I came hither,
  Would I had gone to Paris with John Dory.   240
LUCE
  Farewell, my pretty Nump; I am very sorry
  I cannot bear thee company.
HUMPHREY   Farewell;

234 *confess* acknowledge
234 *quiet* at peace
237 *comfrey* plant common near ditches and streams and supposed to
     have healing virtues
241 *Nump* fool and pet-name for Humphrey

229 *by God's body*. See Interlude I, 11n.
240 *John Dory*. In a song of this title (music by Ravenscroft [1609] reprinted
     in Chappell, i. 93–6) the hero is captured while on his way to the King
     of France with a crew of English 'churls'.

The devil's dam was ne'er so banged in hell.

Exeunt [LUCE *and* JASPER]

Manet HUMPHREY

WIFE

This young Jasper will prove me another thing, o'my
conscience, and he may be suffered. George, dost not see,   245
George, how 'a swaggers, and flies at the very heads o'folks
as he were a dragon? Well, if I do not do his lesson for
wronging the poor gentleman, I am no true woman. His
friends that brought him up might have been better occupied,
iwis, than ha' taught him these fegaries; he's e'en in the   250
highway to the gallows, God bless him.

CITIZEN

You're too bitter, cony; the young man may do well enough
for all this.

WIFE

Come hither, Master Humphrey; has he hurt you? Now
beshrew his fingers for't. Here, sweetheart, here's some   255
green ginger for thee. Now beshrew my heart, but 'a has
peppernel in's head as big as a pullet's egg. Alas, sweet lamb,
how thy temples beat! Take the peace on him, sweetheart,
take the peace on him.

Enter a BOY

CITIZEN

No, no, you talk like a foolish woman. I'll ha' Rafe fight with   260
him, and swinge him up well-favouredly.—Sirrah boy, come
hither; let Rafe come in and fight with Jasper.

WIFE

Ay, and beat him well; he's an unhappy boy.

BOY

Sir, you must pardon us; the plot of our play lies contrary,
and 'twill hazard the spoiling of our play.   265

244 *thing* ed. things Q1
250 *fegaries* vagaries, pranks
257 *peppernel* lump
258 *Take the peace* obtain sureties for his good conduct
261 *swinge* thrash
261 *well-favouredly* handsomely, thoroughly
263 *unhappy* 'mischiefously waggish' (Johnson); cf. *All's Well*, IV.
    v, 67

243 *devil's dam.* Humphrey is probably thinking of a morality play in
    which the devil and his crew were belaboured by the vices.

CITIZEN

Plot me no plots. I'll ha' Rafe come out; I'll make your house
too hot for you else.

BOY

Why, sir, he shall; but if anything fall out of order, the
gentlemen must pardon us.

CITIZEN

Go your ways, goodman boy.   [*Exit* BOY]   270
—I'll hold him a penny he shall have his bellyful of fighting
now. Ho, here comes Rafe; no more.

Enter RAFE, MISTRESS MERRYTHOUGHT, MICHAEL, [TIM *as*]
    Squire, and [GEORGE *as*] *Dwarf*

RAFE

What knight is that, squire? Ask him if he keep
The passage, bound by love of lady fair,
Or else but prickant.   Sir, I am no knight,   275

HUMPHREY

But a poor gentleman, that this same night
Had stolen from me on yonder green
My lovely wife, and suffered (to be seen
Yet extant on my shoulders) such a greeting
That whilst I live I shall think of that meeting.   280

WIFE

Ay, Rafe, he beat him unmercifully, Rafe; and thou spar'st
him, Rafe, I would thou wert hanged.

CITIZEN

No more, wife, no more.

RAFE

Where is the caitiff wretch hath done this deed?
Lady, your pardon, that I may proceed   285
Upon the quest of this injurious knight.
And thou, fair squire, repute me not the worse,
In leaving the great venture of the purse
And the rich casket till some better leisure.

Enter JASPER *and* LUCE

271 *hold* bet
273–4 *keep The passage* guard the entrance to a castle
284 *caitiff* wicked
286 *injurious* malicious

HUMPHREY
Here comes the broker hath purloined my treasure.   290
RAFE
Go, squire, and tell him I am here,
An errant knight at arms, to crave delivery
Of that fair lady to her own knight's arms.
If he deny, bid him take choice of ground,
And so defy him.
TIM   From the knight that bears   295
The golden pestle, I defy thee, knight,
Unless thou make fair restitution
Of that bright lady.

JASPER   Tell the knight that sent thee
He is an ass, and I will keep the wench
And knock his head-piece.
RAFE   Knight, thou art but dead,   300
If thou recall not thy uncourteous terms.
WIFE
Break's pate, Rafe; break's pate, Rafe, soundly.

JASPER
Come, knight, I am ready for you. Now your pestle
                    Snatches away his pestle
Shall try what temper, sir, your mortar's of.
[*Recites*] 'With that he stood upright in his stirrups, and gave   305
the Knight of the Calf-skin such a knock [*Knocks* RAFE *down*]
that he forsook his horse and down he fell; and then he leaped
upon him, and plucking off his helmet—'
HUMPHREY
Nay, and my noble knight be down so soon,
Though I can scarcely go, I needs must run.   310
                    Exeunt HUMPHREY *and* RAFE

WIFE
Run, Rafe; run, Rafe; run for thy life, boy; Jasper comes,
Jasper comes.

290 *broker* pimp   301 *thou* Q2 thou thou Q1
304 *of* Q2 off Q1
305–8 printed as verse in Q1–3, F
310 *go* walk
310 s.d. *Exeunt* ed. *Exit* Q1

306 *Calf-skin.* The old romances were written on calf-skin or vellum.

JASPER
> Come, Luce, we must have other arms for you;
> Humphrey and Golden Pestle, both adieu.   *Exeunt*

WIFE
> Sure the devil, God bless us, is in this springald. Why,   315
> George, didst ever see such a fire-drake? I am afraid my boy's
> miscarried; if he be, though he were Master Merrythought's
> son a thousand times, if there be any law in England, I'll
> make some of them smart for't.

CITIZEN
> No, no, I have found out the matter, sweetheart: Jasper is   320
> enchanted; as sure as we are here, he is enchanted. He could
> no more have stood in Rafe's hands than I can stand in my
> Lord Mayor's. I'll have a ring to discover all enchantments,
> and Rafe shall beat him yet. Be no more vexed, for it shall be
> so.   325

> *Enter* RAFE, [TIM *as*] *Squire,* [GEORGE *as*] *Dwarf,*
> MISTRESS MERRYTHOUGHT *and* MICHAEL

WIFE
> Oh, husband, here's Rafe again.—Stay, Rafe, let me speak
> with thee. How dost thou, Rafe? Art thou not shroadly hurt?
> The foul great lungies laid unmercifully on thee; there's
> some sugar-candy for thee. Proceed, thou shalt have another
> bout with him.   330

CITIZEN
> If Rafe had him at the fencing-school, if he did not make a
> puppy of him, and drive him up and down the school, he
> should ne'er come in my shop more.

MISTRESS MERRYTHOUGHT
> Truly, Master Knight of the Burning Pestle, I am weary.

MICHAEL
> Indeed la, mother, and I am very hungry.   335

RAFE
> Take comfort, gentle dame, and you, fair squire,

315 *springald* stripling
316 *fire-drake* 'A fire sometime seene, flying in the night, like a
     Dragon', J. Bullokar, *An English Expositor* (London, 1616); cf.
     Brand, i. 235
317 *miscarried* come to harm
327 *shroadly* obs. form of shrewdly, grievously
328 *lungies* <Longinus (who speared Christ), louts

For in this desert there must needs be placed
Many strong castles held by courteous knights;
And till I bring you safe to one of those,
I swear by this my order ne'er to leave you.   340

WIFE

Well said, Rafe.—George, Rafe was ever comfortable, was
he not?

CITIZEN

Yes, duck.

WIFE

I shall ne'er forget him, when we had lost our child (you
know it was strayed almost, alone, to Puddle Wharf, and the   345
criers were abroad for it, and there it had drowned itself but
for a sculler), Rafe was the most comfortablest to me: 'Peace,
mistress', says he, 'let it go; I'll get you another as good'. Did
he not, George, did he not say so?

CITIZEN

Yes indeed did he, mouse.   350

GEORGE

I would we had a mess of pottage and a pot of drink, squire,
and were going to bed.

TIM

Why, we are at Waltham town's end, and that's the Bell Inn.

GEORGE

Take courage, valiant knight, damsel, and squire;
I have discovered, not a stone's cast off,   355
An ancient castle held by the old knight
Of the most holy order of the Bell,
Who gives to all knights errant entertain.
There plenty is of food, and all prepared
By the white hands of his own lady dear.   360
He hath three squires that welcome all his guests:
The first hight Chamberlino, who will see
Our beds prepared, and bring us snowy sheets,

---

341 *comfortable* helpful
362 *hight* ed. high Q1, called

---

345 *Puddle Wharf*. A landing place at the foot of St Andrew's Hill, now
    Puddle Dock where the Mermaid Theatre is situated.
354ff. With this episode compare Don Quixote's visit to the Inn on the
    first night of his wanderings, I. ii and iii.

Where never footman stretched his buttered hams;
The second hight Tapstero, who will see   365
Our pots full filled and no froth therein;
The third, a gentle squire, Ostlero hight,
Who will our palfreys slick with wisps of straw,
And in the manger put them oats enough,
And never grease their teeth with candle-snuff.   370

WIFE

That same dwarf's a pretty boy, but the squire's a groutnoll.

RAFE

Knock at the gates, my squire, with stately lance.

Enter TAPSTER

TAPSTER

Who's there?—You're welcome, gentlemen; will you see a
room?

GEORGE

Right courteous and valiant Knight of the Burning Pestle,   375
this is the Squire Tapstero.

RAFE

Fair Squire Tapstero, I, a wandering knight
Hight of the Burning Pestle, in the quest
Of this fair lady's casket and wrought purse,
Losing myself in this vast wilderness,   380
Am to this castle well by fortune brought;
Where, hearing of the goodly entertain
Your knight of holy order of the Bell
Gives to all damsels and all errant knights,
I thought to knock, and now am bold to enter.   385

TAPSTER

An't please you see a chamber, you are very welcome.

Exeunt

WIFE

George, I would have something done, and I cannot tell
what it is.

365 *Tapstero* ed. Tastero Q1; Tapstro Q2–3, F
368 *slick* make sleek   371 *groutnoll* blockhead

364 *Where never . . . hams.* Footmen were servants who ran with their
     master's carriage; they greased their calves to prevent cramp.
370 *never . . . candle-snuff.* A common trick to prevent the horses from
     eating; cf. *King Lear*, II. iv, 124.

CITIZEN
What is it, Nell?

WIFE
Why, George, shall Rafe beat nobody again? Prithee,   390
sweetheart, let him.

CITIZEN
So he shall, Nell; and if I join with him, we'll knock them al!.

Enter HUMPHREY *and* MERCHANT

WIFE
Oh, George, here's Master Humphrey again now, that lost
Mistress Luce, and Mistress Luce's father. Master Humphrey
will do somebody's errand, I warrant him.   395

HUMPHREY
Father, it's true in arms I ne'er shall clasp her,
For she is stol'n away by your man Jasper.

WIFE
I thought he would tell him.

MERCHANT
Unhappy that I am to lose my child!
Now I begin to think on Jasper's words,   400
Who oft hath urged to me thy foolishness.
Why didst thou let her go? Thou lov'st her not,
That wouldst bring home thy life, and not bring her.

HUMPHREY
Father, forgive me. Shall I tell you true?
Look on my shoulders, they are black and blue.   405
Whilst to and fro fair Luce and I were winding,
He came and basted me with a hedge-binding.

MERCHANT
Get men and horses straight; we will be there
Within this hour. You know the place again?

HUMPHREY
I know the place where he my loins did swaddle.   410
I'll get six horses, and to each a saddle.

MERCHANT
Meantime I'll go talk with Jasper's father.   *Exeunt*

---

395 *errand* ed. errant Q1, *do . . . errand* perform a worthy deed
407 *basted* beat
410 *swaddle* swathe, beat soundly

WIFE

George, what wilt thou lay with me now, that Master
Humphrey has not Mistress Luce yet? Speak, George, what
wilt thou lay with me?   415

CITIZEN

No, Nell, I warrant thee Jasper is at Puckeridge with her by
this.

WIFE

Nay, George, you must consider Mistress Luce's feet are
tender, and, besides, 'tis dark; and I promise you truly, I do
not see how he should get out of Waltham Forest with her   420
yet.

CITIZEN

Nay, cony, what wilt thou lay with me that Rafe has her not
yet?

WIFE

I will not lay against Rafe, honey, because I have not spoken
with him. But look, George, peace; here comes the merry   425
old gentleman again.

Enter OLD MERRYTHOUGHT

OLD MERRYTHOUGHT [*sings*]

> *When it was grown to dark midnight,*
> *And all were fast asleep,*
> *In came Margaret's grimly ghost,*
> *And stood at William's feet.*   430

I have money and meat and drink beforehand till tomorrow
at noon; why should I be sad? Methinks I have half a dozen
jovial spirits within me [*sings*]:

> *I am three merry men, and three merry men.*

To what end should any man be sad in this world? Give me   435
a man that when he goes to hanging cries [*sings*]:

413 *lay* wager
429 *grimly* grim-looking

---

416 *Puckeridge.* A village in Hertfordshire, 23 miles N. of London.
427–30 *When it was grown to dark midnight.* A version of a stanza from
   'Fair Margaret and Sweet William', Child No. 74, music in Bronson,
   ii. 155 ff.
434 *I am three merry men.* From a song that appears in Peele's *Old Wives'*
   Tale, and is adapted in III. ii of Fletcher's *The Bloody Brother*; music
   in Chappell, i. 197.

Troll the black bowl to me!
and a woman that will sing a catch in her travail. I have seen
a man come by my door with a serious face, in a black cloak,
without a hat-band, carrying his head as if he looked for pins   440
in the street; I have looked out of my window half a year
after, and have spied that man's head upon London Bridge.
'Tis vile. Never trust a tailor that does not sing at his work:
his mind is of nothing but filching.

WIFE

Mark this, George, 'tis worth noting; Godfrey my tailor,   445
you know, never sings, and he had fourteen yards to make
this gown; and I'll be sworn Mistress Pennistone the draper's
wife had one made with twelve.

OLD MERRYTHOUGHT [*sings*]
    'Tis mirth that fills the veins with blood,
    More than wine, or sleep, or food;   450
    Let each man keep his heart at ease,
    No man dies of that disease.
    He that would his body keep
    From diseases, must not weep;
    But whoever laughs and sings,   455
    Never he his body brings
    Into fevers, gouts, or rheums,
    Or lingeringly his lungs consumes,
    Or meets with achès in the bone,
    Or catarrhs, or griping stone,   460
    But contented lives for aye;
    The more he laughs, the more he may.

---

437 *Troll* pass   438 *catch* song in canon
438 *travail* labour
458 *lungs* Q3 longs Q1
459 *achès* pronounced 'aitches'
460 *griping* suddenly painful

---

437 *Troll the black bowl to me.* A harvest song with this line appears in
    Nashe's *Summer's Last Will and Testament*, ll. 804 ff.; cf. the song
    for the end of *The Shoemakers' Holiday*. Music for a catch to 'Troll
    the bowl to me' is found in Peter Warlock's transcription of *Pammelia
    and other Rounds and Catches by Thomas Ravenscroft* (Oxford, 1928),
    p. 14.
442 *head upon London Bridge.* The heads of traitors were set on poles over
    the bridge gate until the reign of Charles II.

WIFE

Look, George, how say'st thou by this, George? Is't not a
fine old man?—Now God's blessing o'thy sweet lips.—When
wilt thou be so merry, George? Faith, thou art the frowning'st   465
little thing, when thou art angry, in a country.

Enter MERCHANT

CITIZEN

Peace, cony, thou shalt see him taken down too, I warrant
thee. Here's Luce's father come now.

OLD MERRYTHOUGHT [*sings*]
  As you came from Walsingham,
   From that holy land,   470
  There met you not with my true love
   By the way as you came?

MERCHANT

Oh, Master Merrythought, my daughter's gone!
This mirth becomes you not, my daughter's gone.

OLD MERRYTHOUGHT [*sings*]
  Why, an if she be, what care I?   475
  Or let her come, or go, or tarry.

MERCHANT

Mock not my misery; it is your son
Whom I have made my own, when all forsook him,
Has stol'n my only joy, my child, away.

OLD MERRYTHOUGHT [*sings*]
  He set her on a milk-white steed,   480
   And himself upon a grey,
  He never turned his face again,
   But he bore her quite away.

469–72 *As you came from Walsingham.* A very popular ballad that exists in
 many versions (see Hoy, pp. 90–1); music in Chappell, i. 69. Walsingham is a village in Norfolk, and until 1538 was a favourite place of
 pilgrimage to the shrine of the Virgin Mary.

475–6 *Why, an if she be, what care I?* From 'Farewell, Dear Love', a
 popular song that appears in *Twelfth Night*, II. iii, 97 and is given in
 full with music in Robert Jones's *First Book of Songes and Ayres*
 (1600), reprinted in *The English Lute-Songs*, ed. Edmund H. Fellowes,
 revised by Thurston Dart, Series II, Vol. IV (London, 1959), pp. 24–5.

480–3 *He set her on a milk-white steed.* Corresponds to a stanza in 'The
 Ballad of the Knight and the Shepherd's Daughter', No. 110 in the
 Child Collection; music in Bronson, ii. 535 ff. As Child notes, however,
 Merrythought's stanza 'may equally well belong' to the ballad entitled
 'The Douglas Tragedy', Child No. 7; music in Bronson, i. 106 ff.

MERCHANT

    Unworthy of the kindness I have shown
    To thee and thine! Too late I well perceive   485
    Thou art consenting to my daughter's loss.

OLD MERRYTHOUGHT

    Your daughter! what a stir's here wi' yer daughter? Let her
    go, think no more on her, but sing loud. If both my sons were
    on the gallows, I would sing,
            Down, down, down they fall,   490
            Down; and arise they never shall.

MERCHANT

    Oh, might I behold her once again,
    And she once more embrace her aged sire.

OLD MERRYTHOUGHT

    Fie, how scurvily this goes. 'And she once more embrace her
    aged sire'? You'll make a dog on her, will ye? She cares much   495
    for her aged sire, I warrant you. [*sings*]
            She cares not for her daddy, nor
              She cares not for her mammy;
            For she is, she is, she is, she is
              My Lord of Lowgave's lassy.   500

MERCHANT

    For this thy scorn, I will pursue that son
    Of thine to death.

OLD MERRYTHOUGHT

    Do, and when you ha' killed him, [*sings*]
       Give him flowers enow, palmer, give him flowers enow,
       Give him red, and white, and blue, green, and yellow.   505

MERCHANT

    I'll fetch my daughter.

OLD MERRYTHOUGHT

    I'll hear no more o' your daughter; it spoils my mirth.

MERCHANT

    I say, I'll fetch my daughter.

---

487 *wi'* F wee Q1
497 *cares* Q2 cares cares Q1
504 *palmer* pilgrim

490–1 *Down, down, down they fall.* From 'Sorrow Stay,' No. III in John
    Dowland's *The Second Book of Songes and Ayres* (1600), reprinted
    with music in *The English School of Lutenist Song Writers*, ed. E. H.
    Fellowes (London, 1922), First Series, Vol. V, pp. 16–18.
495 *make a dog on her.* Venturewell has called himself Luce's 'sire'.

OLD MERRYTHOUGHT [*sings*]

> Was never man for lady's sake,
>   Down, Down,   510
> Tormented as I, poor Sir Guy,
>   De derry down,
> For Lucy's sake, that lady bright,
>   Down, down,
> As ever men beheld with eye,   515
>   De derry down.

MERCHANT

I'll be revenged, by heaven.   *Exeunt*

Finis Actus secundi

[Interlude II]

Music

WIFE

How dost thou like this, George?

CITIZEN

Why, this is well, cony; but if Rafe were hot once, thou
shouldst see more.

WIFE

The fiddlers go again, husband.

CITIZEN

Ay, Nell, but this is scurvy music. I gave the whoreson   5
gallows money, and I think he has not got me the waits of
Southwark. If I hear 'em not anon, I'll twinge him by the
ears.—You musicians, play 'Baloo'.

WIFE

No, good George, lets ha' 'Lachrimae'.

CITIZEN

Why, this is it, cony.   10

WIFE

It's all the better, George. Now, sweet lamb, what story is

---

7 *'em* ed. him Q1

509–16 *Was never man for lady's sake.* From the legend of Sir Guy, printed
    in Percy's *Reliques*, III. ii.
  8 *'Baloo'.* A word that occurs frequently in the refrains to lullabies; the
    Citizen may be referring to 'Lady Bothwell's Lamentation.'
  9 *'Lachrimae'.* A set of pavanes by Dowland (1605); transcribed by P.
    Warlock (London, 1927).
11–12 *story . . . cloth.* Painted arras cloths, cheap imitations of tapestries,
    hung behind the stage.

that painted upon the cloth? The Confutation of Saint
Paul?

CITIZEN

No, lamb, that's Rafe and Lucrece.

WIFE

Rafe and Lucrece? Which Rafe? Our Rafe?   15

CITIZEN

No, mouse, that was a Tartarian.

WIFE

A Tartarian! Well, I would the fiddlers had done, that we
might see our Rafe again.

[Act III]

Enter JASPER *and* LUCE

JASPER

Come, my dear deer, though we have lost our way,
We have not lost ourselves. Are you not weary
With this night's wandering, broken from your rest,
And frighted with the terror that attends
The darkness of this wild unpeopled place?   5

LUCE

No, my best friend, I cannot either fear
Or entertain a weary thought, whilst you
(The end of all my full desires) stand by me.
Let them that lose their hopes, and live to languish
Amongst the number of forsaken lovers,   10
Tell the long weary steps, and number time,
Start at a shadow, and shrink up their blood,

Act III ed. Actus tertius, Scœna prima Q1
 1 *dear deer* ed. deere deere Q1
 3 *broken* interrupted, roused
 5 *this* Q2 these Q1   11 *Tell* count

12–13 *The Confutation of Saint Paul.* A bawdy malapropism, as Dr T. W.
Craik pointed out to me, for 'the Conversion of Saint Paul'; cf. Fr.
con and Lat. *futuo*.

14 *Rafe and Lucrece.* He means of course 'The Rape of Lucrece', the subject
of Shakespeare's poem and of a play by Heywood printed in 1608.

16 *Tartarian.* Another malapropism for Sextus Tarquinius who raped
Lucrece; the Citizen might however be thinking of the proverbial
cruelty of the inhabitants of Tartary (north of the Caucasus and
Himalayas) towards their women; Tartarian is also a cant name for a
thief.

Whilst I (possessed with all content and quiet)
Thus take my pretty love, and thus embrace him.

JASPER

You have caught me, Luce, so fast, that whilst I live 15
I shall become your faithful prisoner,
And wear these chains for ever. Come, sit down,
And rest your body, too, too delicate
For these disturbances. So, will you sleep?
Come, do not be more able than you are; 20
I know you are not skilful in these watches,
For women are no soldiers; be not nice,
But take it; sleep, I say.

LUCE   I cannot sleep,
Indeed I cannot, friend.

JASPER   Why, then we'll sing,
And try how that will work upon our senses. 25

LUCE

I'll sing, or say, or anything but sleep.

JASPER

Come, little mermaid, rob me of my heart
With that enchanting voice.

LUCE   You mock me, Jasper.

SONG

JASPER *Tell me, dearest, what is love?*
LUCE   *'Tis a lightning from above,* 30
'Tis an arrow, 'tis a fire,
'Tis a boy they call Desire,
        'Tis a smile
        Doth beguile
JASPER *The poor hearts of men that prove.* 35

Tell me more, are women true?
LUCE   *Some love change, and so do you.*
JASPER *Are they fair, and never kind?*
LUCE   *Yes, when men turn with the wind.*
JASPER *Are they froward* 40

17 *wear* Q2 were Q1
22 *nice* reluctant, fastidious
23 *take it* yield   28 SONG Q1ᶜ Sung Q1ᵘ
35 *prove* strive

29–42 *Tell me, dearest, what is love?* The original music for this song has
    survived and is reprinted by E. S. Lindsey, 'The Music of the Songs
    in Fletcher's Plays,' *SP*, XXI (1924), p. 331; the song also occurs
    in *The Captain*, II. ii, 160 ff., with variations and an added stanza.

LUCE   *Ever toward*
Those that love to love anew.

JASPER
   Dissemble it no more; I see the god
   Of heavy sleep lay on his heavy mace
   Upon your eyelids.

LUCE   I am very heavy.   *[Sleeps]*   45

JASPER
   Sleep, sleep, and quiet rest crown thy sweet thoughts.
   Keep from her fair blood distempers, startings,
   Horrors, and fearful shapes; let all her dreams
   Be joys, and chaste delights, embraces, wishes,
   And such new pleasures as the ravished soul   50
   Gives to the senses. So, my charms have took.
   Keep her, you powers divine, whilst I contemplate
   Upon the wealth and beauty of her mind.
   She is only fair and constant, only kind,
   And only to thee, Jasper. Oh my joys,   55
   Whither will you transport me? Let not fullness
   Of my poor buried hopes come up together
   And overcharge my spirits. I am weak.
   Some say (however ill) the sea and women
   Are governed by the moon: both ebb and flow,   60
   Both full of changes. Yet to them that know
   And truly judge, these but opinions are,
   And heresies to bring on pleasing war
   Between our tempers, that without these were
   Both void of after-love, and present fear,   65
   Which are the best of Cupid. Oh thou child
   Bred from despair, I dare not entertain thee,
   Having a love without the faults of women,
   And greater in her perfect goods than men;
   Which to make good, and please myself the stronger,   70

43 *Dissemble it* pretend
45 *heavy* drowsy
47 *distempers* mental or physical disorders
54 *She is only* she alone is
62–6 *opinions . . . Cupid* empty and false notions that pleasantly dis-
   turb the balance of our emotions; for without these we should not
   experience either love in retrospect or the pangs of anxiety which
   are love's chief joys
70 *make good* demonstrate

44 *heavy mace.* The traditional emblem of Morpheus, god of sleep.

Though certainly I am certain of her love,
I'll try her, that the world and memory
May sing to aftertimes her constancy.   [*Draws his sword*]
Luce, Luce, awake.

LUCE   Why do you fright me, friend,
With those distempered looks? What makes your sword   75
Drawn in your hand? Who hath offended you?
I prithee, Jasper, sleep; thou art wild with watching.

JASPER
Come, make your way to heaven, and bid the world
(With all the villainies that stick upon it)
Farewell; you're for another life.

LUCE   Oh Jasper,   80
How have my tender years committed evil
(Especially against the man I love)
Thus to be cropped untimely?

JASPER   Foolish girl,
Canst thou imagine I could love his daughter,
That flung me from my fortune into nothing,   85
Discharged me his service, shut the doors
Upon my poverty, and scorned my prayers,
Sending me, like a boat without a mast,
To sink or swim? Come, by this hand you die;
I must have life and blood to satisfy   90
Your father's wrongs.

WIFE
Away, George, away; raise the watch at Ludgate, and bring
a mittimus from the justice for this desperate villain.—Now
I charge you, gentlemen, see the king's peace kept.—Oh,
my heart, what a varlet's this to offer manslaughter upon the   95
harmless gentlewoman!

CITIZEN
I warrant thee, sweetheart, we'll have him hampered.

LUCE   Oh, Jasper, be not cruel;

72 *try* put to the test
93 *mittimus* warrant for arrest (<Latin 'we send', the first word of
     the writ)   97 *hampered* confined

75ff. In Beaumont and Fletcher's later plays maidens have a distressing
      habit of being wounded by their own lovers' swords.
92 *Ludgate*. Like Newgate, it was used as a prison and a station for the
      watch.

If thou wilt kill me, smile and do it quickly,
And let not many deaths appear before me.   100
I am a woman made of fear and love,
A weak, weak woman; kill not with thy eyes,
They shoot me through and through. Strike, I am ready;
And, dying, still I love thee.

Enter MERCHANT, HUMPHREY, *and his men*

MERCHANT   Whereabouts?
JASPER [*Aside*]
No more of this, now to myself again.   105
HUMPHREY
There, there he stands with sword, like martial knight,
Drawn in his hand; therefore beware the fight,
You that be wise; for, were I good Sir Bevis,
I would not stay his coming, by your leaves.
MERCHANT
Sirrah, restore my daughter.
JASPER   Sirrah, no.   110
MERCHANT
Upon him, then.

WIFE
So, down with him, down with him, down with him! Cut
him i'th' leg, boys, cut him i'th' leg!

MERCHANT
Come your ways, minion. I'll provide a cage
For you, you're grown so tame.—Horse her away.   115
HUMPHREY
Truly I'm glad your forces have the day.

Exeunt, manet JASPER

JASPER
They are gone, and I am hurt; my love is lost,
Never to get again. Oh, me unhappy,
Bleed, bleed, and die! I cannot. Oh my folly,
Thou hast betrayed me! Hope, where art thou fled?   120
Tell me if thou be'st anywhere remaining.

109 *stay* await   114 *minion* hussy

104 *Whereabouts?* The incongruity of Venturewell's 'reply' to Luce's
   declamation is intentional.
108 *Sir Bevis.* The hero of Sir Bevis of Hampton, a famous medieval
   romance.

Shall I but see my love again? Oh, no!
She will not deign to look upon her butcher,
Nor is it fit she should; yet I must venture.
Oh, chance, or fortune, or whate'er thou art   125
That men adore for powerful, hear my cry,
And let me loving live, or losing die.   *Exit*

WIFE
 Is'a gone, George?
CITIZEN
 Ay, cony.
WIFE
 Marry, and let him go, sweetheart. By the faith o' my body,   130
 'a has put me into such a fright that I tremble, as they say,
 as 'twere an aspen leaf. Look o' my little finger, George, how
 it shakes. Now, i'truth, every member of my body is the worse
 for't.
CITIZEN
 Come, hug in mine arms, sweet mouse; he shall not fright   135
 thee any more. Alas, mine own dear heart, how it quivers.

Enter MISTRESS MERRYTHOUGHT, RAFE, MICHAEL, [TIM *as*] *Squire,*
    [GEORGE *as*] *Dwarf,* HOST, *and a* TAPSTER

WIFE
 Oh, Rafe, how dost thou, Rafe? How hast thou slept tonight?
 Has the knight used thee well?
CITIZEN
 Peace, Nell; let Rafe alone.

TAPSTER
 Master, the reckoning is not paid.   140
RAFE
 Right courteous knight, who, for the order's sake
 Which thou hast ta'en, hang'st out the holy bell,
 As I this flaming pestle bear about,
 We render thanks to your puissant self,
 Your beauteous lady, and your gentle squires,   145
 For thus refreshing of our wearied limbs,
 Stiffened with hard achievements in wild desert.
TAPSTER
 Sir, there is twelve shillings to pay.

137 *tonight* last night

148 *twelve shillings.* The bill is not exorbitant.

RAFE

Thou merry squire Tapstero, thanks to thee
For comforting our souls with double jug;   150
And if advent'rous fortune prick thee forth,
Thou jovial squire, to follow feats of arms,
Take heed thou tender every lady's cause,
Every true knight, and every damsel fair;
But spill the blood of treacherous Saracens   155
And false enchanters that with magic spells
Have done to death full many a noble knight.

HOST

Thou valiant Knight of the Burning Pestle, give ear to me:
there is twelve shillings to pay, and as I am a true knight, I
will not bate a penny.   160

WIFE

George, I pray thee tell me, must Rafe pay twelve shillings
now?

CITIZEN

No, Nell, no; nothing but the old knight is merry with Rafe.

WIFE

Oh, is't nothing else? Rafe will be as merry as he.

RAFE

Sir knight, this mirth of yours becomes you well;   165
But to requite this liberal courtesy,
If any of your squires will follow arms,
He shall receive from my heroic hand
A knighthood, by the virtue of this pestle.

HOST

Fair knight, I thank you for your noble offer;   170
Therefore, gentle knight,
Twelve shillings you must pay, or I must cap you.

150 *double jug* strong ale
151 *advent'rous* hazardous
151 *prick thee forth* spur you on
153 *tender* support
154 *Every true knight, and every damsel fair* Q2 Euery truery **true**
    Knight, and euery damsell faire faire Q1
160 *bate* deduct
171 The sense is incomplete and presumably some words have
    dropped out
172 *cap* seize, arrest

---

155 *Saracens.* The Mahommedan enemies of the Crusaders; but the
description is applied loosely to the villains of the romances.

WIFE

Look, George, did not I tell thee as much; the Knight of the
Bell is in earnest. Rafe shall not be beholding to him; give
him his money, George, and let him go snick up.   175

CITIZEN

Cap Rafe? No.—Hold your hand, Sir Knight of the Bell;
there's your money. Have you anything to say to Rafe now?
Cap Rafe!

WIFE

I would you should know it, Rafe has friends that will not
suffer him to be capped for ten times so much, and ten times   180
to the end of that.—Now take thy course, Rafe.

MISTRESS MERRYTHOUGHT

Come, Michael, thou and I will go home to thy father; he
hath enough left to keep us a day or two, and we'll set fellows
abroad to cry our purse and our casket. Shall we, Michael?

MICHAEL

Ay, I pray, mother. In truth my feet are full of chilblains with   185
travelling.

WIFE

Faith, and those chilblains are a foul trouble. Mistress
Merrythought, when your youth comes home, let him rub
all the soles of his feet and the heels and his ankles with a
mouse skin; or, if none of your people can catch a mouse,   190
when he goes to bed let him roll his feet in the warm embers,
and I warrant you he shall be well; and you may make him
put his fingers between his toes and smell to them; it's very
sovereign for his head if he be costive.

MISTRESS MERRYTHOUGHT

Master Knight of the Burning Pestle, my son Michael and I   195
bid you farewell; I thank your worship heartily for your
kindness.

RAFE

Farewell, fair lady, and your tender squire.
If, pricking through these deserts, I do hear

174 *beholding* vulgarism for 'beholden'
184 *cry* announce loss of
194 *sovereign* good
194 *costive* constipated

Of any traitorous knight who through his guile   200
Hath light upon your casket and your purse,
I will despoil him of them and restore them.
MISTRESS MERRYTHOUGHT
I thank your worship.   *Exit with* MICHAEL
RAFE
Dwarf, bear my shield; squire, elevate my lance;
And now farewell, you Knight of holy Bell.   205

CITIZEN
Ay, ay, Rafe, all is paid.

RAFE
But yet before I go, speak, worthy knight,
If aught you do of sad adventures know,
Where errant knight may through his prowess win
Eternal fame, and free some gentle souls   210
From endless bonds of steel and ling'ring pain.
HOST [*to* TAPSTER]
Sirrah, go to Nick the barber, and bid him prepare himself
as I told you before, quickly.
TAPSTER
I am gone, sir.   *Exit* TAPSTER
HOST
Sir knight, this wilderness affordeth none   215
But the great venture where full many a knight
Hath tried his prowess and come off with shame,
And where I would not have you lose your life
Against no man, but furious fiend of hell.
RAFE
Speak on, sir knight, tell what he is and where;   220
For here I vow upon my blazing badge,
Never to blaze a day in quietness;
But bread and water will I only eat,
And the green herb and rock shall be my couch,
Till I have quelled that man or beast or fiend   225
That works such damage to all errant knights.

208 *sad* grave
209 *knight* ed. knights Q1
222 *blaze* probably caught from 'blazing' above; Dyce suggested 'lose'
    or 'pass'
225 *quelled* slain

212 *Nick.* Don Quixote's barber was called Master Nicholas, I.v.

HOST

Not far from hence, near to a craggy cliff,
At the north end of this distressed town,
There doth stand a lowly house
Ruggedly builded, and in it a cave   230
In which an ugly giant now doth won,
Ycleped Barbaroso. In his hand
He shakes a naked lance of purest steel,
With sleeves turned up, and him before he wears
A motley garment to preserve his clothes   235
From blood of those knights which he massacres,
And ladies gent. Without his door doth hang
A copper basin on a prickant spear,
At which no sooner gentle knights can knock
But the shrill sound fierce Barbaroso hears,   240
And rushing forth, brings in the errant knight,
And sets him down in an enchanted chair.
Then with an engine which he hath prepared,
With forty teeth, he claws his courtly crown;
Next makes him wink, and underneath his chin   245
He plants a brazen pece of mighty bord,
And knocks his bullets round about his cheeks,
Whilst with his fingers, and an instrument
With which he snaps his hair off, he doth fill
The wretch's ears with a most hideous noise.   250
Thus every knight adventurer he doth trim,
And now no creature dares encounter him.

231 *ugly* fearsome   231 *won* dwell
232 *Ycleped* named
232 *Barbaroso* for Barbarossa (see III, 323)
237 *gent* fair
238 *prickant* pointing upward
239 *can* do   246 *pece* cup
246 *bord* rim
247 *bullets* small balls of soap
251 *trim* often used figuratively meaning to thrash or trounce

238 *copper basin on a prickant spear*. The sign of the barber-surgeon; the
     pole was painted red and white and together with the basin signified
     that the barber not only cut hair but drew teeth and let blood.
245 *wink*. For the purpose of anointing his eyes with perfumed water, see
     III, 378.
249 *snaps his hair off*. The long hair affected by gallants was often satirized—
     see III, 377 below; Beaumont's *The Woman Hater*, V. iv, 165; Dekker's
     Gull's Hornbook, Ch. iii; and Stubbes, i. 67–9.

RAFE

In God's name, I will fight with him. Kind sir,
Go but before me to this dismal cave
Where this huge giant Barbaroso dwells,   255
And, by that virtue that brave Rosicleer
That damned brood of ugly giants slew,
And Palmerin Frannarco overthrew,
I doubt not but to curb this traitor foul,
And to the devil send his guilty soul.   260

HOST

Brave sprighted knight, thus far I will perform
This your request: I'll bring you within sight
Of this most loathsome place, inhabited
By a more loathsome man; but dare not stay,
For his main force swoops all he sees away.   265

RAFE

Saint George, set on before! March, squire and page.

Exeunt

WIFE

George, dost think Rafe will confound the giant?

CITIZEN

I hold my cap to a farthing he does. Why, Nell, I saw him
wrestle with the great Dutchman and hurl him.

WIFE

Faith, and that Dutchman was a goodly man, if all things   270
were answerable to his bigness; and yet they say there was a
Scotchman higher than he, and that they two and a knight
met and saw one another for nothing; but of all the sights

253 *with* Q2 (om. Q1)
256 *virtue that* virtue with which; 'that' is to be understood again be-
    fore 'Palmerin' in l. 258
265 *main* full, sheer
265 *swoops* Q2 soopes Q1

257 *damned brood of ugly giants.* Rafe has in mind Rosicleer's adventure
    with the giant Brandagedeon and his thirty knights, told in *The
    Mirror of Knighthood*, I. xxxvi (Murch).
258 *Frannarco.* The account of how Palmerin slew the giant Frannarco
    is found in *Palmerin d'Oliva*, I. li—the chapter from which Rafe read
    in I, 214 ff.
269 *Dutchman.* For the Elizabethans 'Dutchmen' included speakers of both
    High and Low German. It is impossible to identify for certain whom
    the Wife refers to—Sugden gives references to a huge German fencer
    who lived in London, pp. 164 and 221; see also Murch, p. 199.

that ever were in London since I was married, methinks the
little child that was so fair grown about the members was   275
the prettiest, that and the hermaphrodite.

CITIZEN

Nay, by your leave, Nell, Ninivie was better.

WIFE

Ninivie? Oh, that was the story of Joan and the wall, was it
not, George?

CITIZEN

Yes, lamb.   280

Enter MISTRESS MERRYTHOUGHT

WIFE

Look, George, here comes Mistress Merrythought again,
and I would have Rafe come and fight with the giant. I tell
you true, I long to see't.

CITIZEN

Good Mistress Merrythought, begone, I pray you, for my
sake. I pray you, forbear a little; you shall have audience   285
presently; I have a little business.

WIFE

Mistress Merrythought, if it please you to refrain your
passion a little till Rafe have dispatched the giant out of the
way, we shall think ourselves much bound to you. I thank
you, good Mistress Merrythought.   290

Exit MISTRESS MERRYTHOUGHT

Enter a BOY

CITIZEN

Boy, come hither; send away Rafe and this whoreson giant
quickly.

BOY

In good faith, sir, we cannot. You'll utterly spoil our play,
and make it to be hissed, and it cost money; you will not
suffer us to go on with our plot.—I pray, gentlemen, rule   295
him.

---

288 *dispatched* Q2 dispatch Q1
291 *away* along

---

275 *little child*. Like Jonson, Beaumont is satirizing the citizens' taste for
freaks—cf. *The Alchemist*, V. i, 21 ff.
277 *Ninivie*. 'Nineveh, with Jonas and the Whale' was an extremely
popular motion (puppet play) of the time. (Jonah preached in Nineveh
after escaping from the whale.)

CITIZEN

Let him come now and dispatch this, and I'll trouble you no
more.

BOY

Will you give me your hand of that?

WIFE

Give him thy hand, George, do, and I'll kiss him. I warrant   300
thee the youth means plainly.

BOY

I'll send him to you presently.   *Exit* BOY

WIFE

I thank you, little youth.—Faith, the child hath a sweet
breath, George, but I think it be troubled with the worms.
Carduus benedictus and mare's milk were the only thing in   305
the world for't. Oh, Rafe's here, George.—God send thee
good luck, Rafe.

Enter RAFE, HOST, [TIM *as*] *Squire, and* [GEORGE *as*] *Dwarf*

HOST

Puissant knight, yonder his mansion is;
Lo, where the spear and copper basin are;
Behold that string on which hangs many a tooth   310
Drawn from the gentle jaw of wandering knights.
I dare not stay to sound; he will appear.   *Exit* HOST

RAFE

Oh, faint not, heart. Susan, my lady dear,
The cobbler's maid in Milk Street, for whose sake
I take these arms, oh let the thought of thee   315
Carry thy knight through all adventurous deeds,
And in the honour of thy beauteous self
May I destroy this monster Barbaroso.—
Knock, squire, upon the basin till it break
With the shrill strokes, or till the giant speak.   320

Enter BARBER

301 *plainly* honestly
302 *presently* immediately
305 *Carduus benedictus* the blessed thistle, used as a panacea
312 *sound* blow a horn

305 *mare's milk*. Mare's milk was considered useful for purging (Murch).
313ff. The incidents in this contest, the invocation of the lady (Susan is the
    equivalent of Don Quixote's Dulcinea), the formal challenge, the
    hero's magnanimity, etc., are parodies of conventions in the romances.
314 *Milk Street*. Ran north from Cheapside.

WIFE

Oh, George, the giant, the giant!—Now, Rafe, for thy life.

BARBER

What fond unknowing wight is this that dares
So rudely knock at Barbarossa's cell,
Where no man comes but leaves his fleece behind?

RAFE

I, traitorous caitiff, who am sent by fate   325
To punish all the sad enormities
Thou hast committed against ladies gent
And errant knights. Traitor to God and men,
Prepare thyself; this is the dismal hour
Appointed for thee to give strict account   330
Of all thy beastly treacherous villainies.

BARBER

Foolhardy knight, full soon thou shalt aby
                                        He takes down his pole
This fond reproach: thy body will I bang,
And, lo, upon that string thy teeth shall hang.
Prepare thyself, for dead soon shalt thou be.   335

RAFE

Saint George for me!

BARBER

Gargantua for me!   *They fight*

WIFE

To him, Rafe, to him! Hold up the giant; set out thy leg
before, Rafe.

CITIZEN

Falsify a blow, Rafe; falsify a blow; the giant lies open on the   340
left side.

---

322 *fond* foolish   322 *wight* man
324 *fleece* pun meaning hair and money (cf. 'to fleece someone')
325 *caitiff* wretch, rogue   332 *aby* pay for
337 s.d. Q1 prints on line 336   340 *Falsify* feign

---

334 *string.* Drawn teeth were hung on a string outside the barber's shop;
  cf. *The Woman Hater*, III. iii, 109–10.
337 *Gargantua.* More probably the hero of the folk-tale than of Rabelais'
  work which was little known in England at this date—see *Every Man
  in his Humour* (1616), III. ii, 25, and Herford and Simpson's note
  (ix, 362).

WIFE

Bear't off; bear't off still. There, boy.—Oh, Rafe's almost
down, Rafe's almost down.

RAFE

Susan, inspire me.—Now have up again.

WIFE

Up, up, up, up, up! So, Rafe, down with him, down with   345
him, Rafe.

CITIZEN

Fetch him o'er the hip, boy.

WIFE

There, boy; kill, kill, kill, kill, kill, Rafe.

CITIZEN

No, Rafe, get all out of him first.

[RAFE *knocks the* BARBER *down*]

RAFE

Presumptuous man, see to what desperate end   350
Thy treachery hath brought thee. The just gods,
Who never prosper those that do despise them,
For all the villainies which thou hast done
To knights and ladies, now have paid thee home
By my stiff arm, a knight adventurous.   355
But say, vile wretch, before I send thy soul
To sad Avernus, whither it must go,
What captives hold'st thou in thy sable cave?

BARBER

Go in and free them all; thou hast the day.

RAFE

Go, squire and dwarf, search in this dreadful cave,   360
And free the wretched prisoners from their bonds.

Exeunt [TIM *as*] *Squire and* [GEORGE *as*] *Dwarf*

BARBER

I crave for mercy, as thou art a knight,
And scorn'st to spill the blood of those that beg.

---

354 *paid . . . home* fully punished
358 *sable* black

---

357 *Avernus.* Lake Avernus, near Naples; its gloomy appearance gave rise
   to the belief that it was an entrance to the underworld.

RAFE
>   Thou show'd'st no mercy, nor shalt thou have any;
>   Prepare thyself, for thou shalt surely die.   365

>   *Enter* [TIM *as*]
>   *Squire leading one winking, with a basin under his chin*

TIM
>   Behold, brave knight, here is one prisoner,
>   Whom this wild man hath usèd as you see.

WIFE
>   This is the first wise word I heard the squire speak.

RAFE
>   Speak what thou art, and how thou hast been used,
>   That I may give him condign punishment.   370

1 KNIGHT
>   I am a knight that took my journey post
>   Northward from London, and in courteous wise
>   This giant trained me to his loathsome den
>   Under pretence of killing of the itch;
>   And all my body with a powder strewed,   375
>   That smarts and stings, and cut away my beard
>   And my curled locks wherein were ribands tied,
>   And with a water washed my tender eyes
>   (Whilst up and down about me still he skipped),
>   Whose virtue is, that till mine eyes be wiped   380
>   With a dry cloth, for this my foul disgrace
>   I shall not dare to look a dog i'th' face.

WIFE
>   Alas, poor knight.—Relieve him, Rafe; relieve poor knights
>   whilst you live.

RAFE
>   My trusty squire, convey him to the town,   385
>   Where he may find relief.—Adieu, fair knight.

>   *Exit* KNIGHT [*with* TIM, *who presently re-enters*]

365 s.d. *winking* with his eyes shut
370 *That . . . condign* Q2 That that I may giue condigne Q1
370 *condign* appropriate
371 *post* in haste   373 *trained* lured

---

374 *itch*. The result of sexual excess; cf. *The Wild-Goose Chase*, I. i.:
'They cannot rub off old friends, their French itches.'

Enter [GEORGE *as*]
Dwarf leading one with a patch o'er his nose

GEORGE
　Puissant Knight of the Burning Pestle hight,
　See here another wretch, whom this foul beast
　Hath scorched and scored in this inhuman wise.

RAFE
　Speak me thy name and eke thy place of birth,   390
　And what hath been thy usage in this cave.

2 KNIGHT
　I am a knight, Sir Pockhole is my name,
　And by my birth I am a Londoner,
　Free by my copy; but my ancestors
　Were Frenchmen all; and riding hard this way   395
　Upon a trotting horse, my bones did ache;
　And I, faint knight, to ease my weary limbs,
　Light at this cave, when straight this furious fiend,
　With sharpest instrument of purest steel
　Did cut the gristle of my nose away,   400
　And in the place this velvet plaster stands.
　Relieve me, gentle knight, out of his hands.

WIFE
　Good Rafe, relieve Sir Pockhole and send him away, for,
　in truth, his breath stinks.

RAFE
　Convey him straight after the other knight.—   405
　Sir Pockhole, fare you well.
2 KNIGHT   Kind sir, goodnight.

Exit [KNIGHT *with* GEORGE, *who presently re-enters*]
Cries within

3 KNIGHT
　Deliver us.

389 *scorched* slashed with a knife
394 *copy* certificate of admission to the freedom of the City

386 s.d. *patch o'er his nose*. He is suffering from an advanced stage of the
　　French pox or syphilis that eventually attacks the bones.
401 *velvet plaster*. Velvet patches were used to cover both honourable
　　scars and the incisions made to relieve venereal disease; cf. *All's Well*,
　　IV, v, 85.

WOMAN
  Deliver us.

WIFE
  Hark, George, what a woeful cry there is. I think some
  woman lies in there.   410

3 KNIGHT
  Deliver us.
WOMAN
  Deliver us.
RAFE
  What ghastly noise is this? Speak, Barbaroso,
  Or by this blazing steel thy head goes off.
BARBER
  Prisoners of mine, whom I in diet keep.   415
  Send lower down into the cave,
  And in a tub that's heated smoking hot,
  There may they find them and deliver them.
RAFE
  Run, squire and dwarf, deliver them with speed.
                    Exeunt [TIM *as*] *Squire and* [GEORGE *as*] *Dwarf*

WIFE
  But will not Rafe kill this giant? Surely I am afeared if he let   420
  him go he will do as much hurt as ever he did.
CITIZEN
  Not so, mouse, neither, if he could convert him.
WIFE
  Ay, George, if he could convert him; but a giant is not so
  soon converted as one of us ordinary people. There's a pretty
  tale of a witch that had the devil's mark about her, God bless   425
  us, that had a giant to her son, that was called Lob-lie-by-
  the-fire; didst never hear it, George?

411 s.p. 3 KNIGHT throughout the scene, the Third Knight's
    speeches are prefixed MAN in Q1–3, F

---

417 *tub.* Sweating-tubs were used as a cure for the pox; cf. *Timon of Athens*,
    IV. iii, 86.
425 *devil's mark.* Witches were supposed to be branded by the devil.
426–7 *Lob-lie-by-the-fire.* Little is known of this creature—see J. H. Ewing,
    Lob-lie-by-the-fire (London, 1937) and cf. *The Faerie Queene*, III.
    vii, 12, the canto in which the Squire of Dames (see II, 168 n.) also
    appears

Enter [TIM *as*] *Squire leading a man with a glass of lotion in*
his hand, and [GEORGE *as*] *the Dwarf leading a woman with*
diet-bread and drink

CITIZEN
Peace, Nell, here comes the prisoners.

GEORGE
Here be these pinèd wretches, manful knight,
That for these six weeks have not seen a wight.   430

RAFE
Deliver what you are, and how you came
To this sad cave, and what your usage was.

3 KNIGHT
I am an errant knight that followed arms
With spear and shield, and in my tender years
I stricken was with Cupid's fiery shaft,   435
And fell in love with this my lady dear,
And stole her from her friends in Turnbull Street,
And bore her up and down from town to town
Where we did eat and drink and music hear,
Till at the length, at this unhappy town   440
We did arrive, and coming to this cave,
This beast us caught and put us in a tub
Where we this two months sweat, and should have done
Another month if you had not relieved us.

WOMAN
This bread and water hath our diet been,   445
Together with a rib cut from a neck
Of burnèd mutton; hard hath been our fare.
Release us from this ugly giant's snare.

3 KNIGHT
This hath been all the food we have received;
But only twice a day, for novelty,   450
He gave a spoonful of this hearty broth   *Pulls out a syringe*
To each of us, through this same slender quill.

427 s.d. *diet-bread* special bread for syphilitics
429 *pinèd* starved, wasted
431 *Deliver* state
451 *hearty* strengthening

437 *Turnbull Street*. Originally Turnmill Street, it runs south from
Clerkenwell Green. It was a notorious haunt of prostitutes, cf. *2 Henry
IV*, III. ii, 295, etc.

RAFE
From this infernal monster you shall go,
That useth knights and gentle ladies so.—
Convey them hence. 455

Exeunt [3 KNIGHT] *and* WOMAN [*with* TIM *and* GEORGE *who
presently re-enter*]

CITIZEN
Cony, I can tell thee the gentlemen like Rafe.
WIFE
Ay, George, I see it well enough.—Gentlemen, I thank you
all heartily for gracing my man Rafe, and I promise you you
shall see him oft'ner.

BARBER
Mercy, great knight, I do recant my ill, 460
And henceforth never gentle blood will spill.
RAFE
I give thee mercy; but yet shalt thou swear
Upon my burning pestle to perform
Thy promise uttered.
BARBER
I swear and kiss.
RAFE   Depart then, and amend.— 465
                                    [*Exit* BARBER]
Come, squire and dwarf, the sun grows towards his set,
And we have many more adventures yet.   *Exeunt*

CITIZEN
Now Rafe is in this humour, I know he would ha' beaten
all the boys in the house if they had been set on him.
WIFE
Ay, George, but it is well as it is; I warrant you the gentlemen 470
do consider what it is to overthrow a giant. But look, George,
here comes Mistress Merrythought and her son Michael.—
Now you are welcome, Mistress Merrythought, now Rafe
has done, you may go on.

Enter MISTRESS MERRYTHOUGHT *and* MICHAEL

MISTRESS MERRYTHOUGHT
Mick, my boy. 475
MICHAEL
Ay, forsooth, mother.

MISTRESS MERRYTHOUGHT

Be merry, Mick; we are at home now, where, I warrant you,
you shall find the house flung out at the windows.

                                   [Music within]
Hark, hey dogs, hey; this is the old world, i'faith, with my
husband. If I get in among 'em, I'll play 'em such a lesson   480
that they shall have little list to come scraping hither again.
—Why, Master Merrythought, husband, Charles Merrythought.

OLD MERRYTHOUGHT (*[sings] within*)
      If you will sing and dance and laugh,
        And hollo and laugh again,   485
    And then cry, 'There, boys, there', why then
        One, two, three, and four,
      We shall be merry within this hour.

MISTRESS MERRYTHOUGHT

Why, Charles, do you not know your own natural wife? I say,
open the door, and turn me out those mangy companions;   490
'tis more than time that they were fellow and fellow-like with
you. You are a gentleman, Charles, and an old man, and
father of two children; and I myself (though I say it) by my
mother's side niece to a worshipful gentleman, and a
conductor; he has been three times in his majesty's service   495
at Chester, and is now the fourth time, God bless him and
his charge, upon his journey.

OLD MERRYTHOUGHT [*sings within*]
      Go from my window, love, go;
      Go from my window, my dear;
        The wind and the rain   500
        Will drive you back again;
      You cannot be lodged here.

Hark you, Mistress Merrythought, you that walk upon

---

478 *the house . . . windows* a scene of roisterous merry-making
    (Tilley, H 785)
479 *world* habit
483 s.d. *within* Merrythought probably appeared at the window
    stage above, as can be deduced from ll. 498 & 562; cf. Smith,
    pp. 375 ff.
485 *hollo* shout
495 *conductor* captain

498ff. and 516ff. *Go from my window, love, go.* A popular song that appears
    also in *Monsieur Thomas*, III. iii, *The Woman's Prize*, I. iii, and
    Heywood's *The Rape of Lucrece*; music in Chappell, i. 146.

adventures and forsake your husband because he sings with
never a penny in his purse; what, shall I think myself the   505
worse? Faith, no, I'll be merry. You come out here; here's
none but lads of mettle, lives of a hundred years and upwards;
care never drunk their bloods, nor want made 'em warble,
                                                    [*sings*]
          Heigh-ho, my heart is heavy.

MISTRESS MERRYTHOUGHT
Why, Master Merrythought, what am I that you should   510
laugh me to scorn thus abruptly? Am I not your fellow-
feeler, as we may say, in all our miseries, your comforter in
health and sickness? Have I not brought you children? Are
they not like you, Charles? Look upon thine own image,
hard-hearted man. And yet for all this—   515

OLD MERRYTHOUGHT ([*sings*] *within*)

          Begone, begone, my Juggy, my puggy,
          Begone, my love, my dear.
              The weather is warm
              'Twill do thee no harm
              Thou canst not be lodged here.   520

—Be merry, boys; some light music, and more wine.

WIFE
He's not in earnest, I hope, George, is he?

CITIZEN
What if he be, sweetheart?

WIFE
Marry, if he be, George, I'll make bold to tell him he's an
ingrant old man to use his bed-fellow so scurvily.   525

CITIZEN
What, how does he use her, honey?

WIFE
Marry come up, Sir Saucebox, I think you'll take his part,
will you not? Lord, how hot you are grown. You are a fine
man, an you had a fine dog; it becomes you sweetly.

CITIZEN
Nay, prithee, Nell, chide not. For as I am an honest man and   530
a true Christian grocer, I do not like his doings.

---

507 *lives . . . upwards* their merry lives have kept them young
516 *Juggy* diminutive of Joan
516 *puggy* term of endearment   524 *Marry* indeed
525 *ingrant* ignorant, ill-mannered
527 *Marry come up* a taunt = 'now, now'

WIFE

I cry you mercy then, George. You know we are all frail and
full of infirmities.—D'ee hear, Master Merrythought, may I
crave a word with you?

OLD MERRYTHOUGHT (*within*)

Strike up lively, lads.   535

WIFE

I had not thought, in truth, Master Merrythought, that a
man of your age and discretion, as I may say, being a gentleman, and therefore known by your gentle conditions, could
have used so little respect to the weakness of his wife. For your
wife is your own flesh, the staff of your age, your yoke-fellow,   540
with whose help you draw through the mire of this transitory
world. Nay, she's your own rib. And again—

OLD MERRYTHOUGHT ([*sings*] *within*)

  I come not hither for thee to teach,
  I have no pulpit for thee to preach,
  I would thou hadst kissed me under the breech,   545
  As thou art a lady gay.

WIFE

Marry, with a vengeance! I am heartily sorry for the poor
gentlewoman.—But if I were thy wife, i'faith, grey-beard,
i'faith—

CITIZEN

I prithee, sweet honeysuckle, be content.   550

WIFE

Give me such words that am a gentlewoman born! Hang him,
hoary rascal! Get me some drink, George, I am almost molten
with fretting: now beshrew his knave's heart for it.

                                            [*Exit* CITIZEN]

OLD MERRYTHOUGHT [*within*]

Play me a light lavolta. Come, be frolic. Fill the good fellows'
wine.   555

MISTRESS MERRYTHOUGHT

Why, Master Merrythought, are you disposed to make me
wait here? You'll open, I hope; I'll fetch them that shall open
else.

532 *cry you mercy* beg your pardon   538 *conditions* qualities
540 *yoke-fellow* companion at the plough
554 *lavolta* a lively dance for two people   554 *frolic*·merry

OLD MERRYTHOUGHT [*within*]
Good woman, if you will sing I'll give you something; if not—

SONG

You are no love for me, Marg'ret,   560
I am no love for you.

Come aloft, boys, aloft.

MISTRESS MERRYTHOUGHT
Now a churl's fart in your teeth, sir.—Come, Mick, we'll not
trouble him; 'a shall not ding us i'th'teeth with his bread and
his broth, that he shall not. Come, boy; I'll provide for thee,   565
I warrant thee. We'll go to Master Venturewell's, the merchant; I'll get his letter to mine host of the Bell in Waltham;
there I'll place thee with the tapster. Will not that do well for
thee, Mick? And let me alone for that old cuckoldly knave
your father; I'll use him in his kind, I warrant ye.   570

[*Exeunt*]

Finis actus tertii

[Interlude III]

Music [*Enter* BOY]

[*Enter* CITIZEN]

WIFE
Come, George, where's the beer?

CITIZEN
Here, love.

WIFE
This old fornicating fellow will not out of my mind yet.—
Gentlemen, I'll begin to you all, and I desire more of your
acquaintance, with all my heart. [*Drinks*] Fill the gentlemen   5
some beer, George.

BOY *danceth*

562 *Come . . . aloft* printed as part of preceding song in Q1–3, F
564 *ding* strike, i.e. taunt
570 *in his kind* as he deserves
570 s.d. *Finis . . . Music* printed below line 6 of following interlude
    in Q1–3, F
  4 *begin to* toast

560–61 *You are no love for me, Marg'ret.* Probably a fragment of some
    version of the ballad of Fair Margaret and Sweet William—see II,
    427 n.
562 *Come aloft.* 'The expression is generally found applied to apes that were
    taught to vault: here it is used merely as an incitement to mirth' (Dyce).

Look, George, the little boy's come again; methinks he looks
something like the Prince of Orange in his long stocking, if
he had a little harness about his neck. George, I will have him
dance 'Fading'.—'Fading' is a fine jig, I'll assure you, gentle-   10
men.—Begin, brother.—Now 'a capers, sweetheart.—Now a
turn o'th'toe, and then tumble. Cannot you tumble, youth?

BOY

No, indeed, forsooth.

WIFE

Nor eat fire?

BOY

Neither.   15

WIFE

Why then, I thank you heartily. There's twopence to buy you
points withal.   [*Exit* BOY]

[Act IV]

Enter JASPER *and* [*a*] BOY

JASPER [*gives a letter*]
There, boy, deliver this, but do it well.
Hast thou provided me four lusty fellows
Able to carry me? and art thou perfect
In all thy business?

BOY   Sir, you need not fear:
I have my lesson here and cannot miss it.   5
The men are ready for you, and what else
Pertains to this employment.

JASPER [*gives him money*]   There, my boy;
Take it, but buy no land.

---

9 *harness* armour
10 *Fading* an Irish dance, also the act of love (see Partridge)
17 *points* tagged laces for tying hose to doublet
   Act IV ed. Q1–3, F print 'Actus Quartus, Scœna prima' above
   s.d. 'BOY *danceth*' of preceding interlude
1–2 printed as prose in Q1
2 *lusty* vigorous
3 *perfect* instructed
8 *buy no land* cf. the proverb 'he that buys land buys many stones'
   (Tilley, L 52)

---

8 *Prince of Orange*. Probably a reference to a well-known picture of Prince
   Maurice, son of William of Orange.

BOY   Faith, sir, 'twere rare
  To see so young a purchaser. I fly,
  And on my wings carry your destiny.   *Exit*   10

JASPER
  Go, and be happy.—Now, my latest hope,
  Forsake me not, but fling thy anchor out
  And let it hold. Stand fixed, thou rolling stone,
  Till I enjoy my dearest. Hear me, all
  You powers that rule in men celestial.   *Exit*   15

WIFE
  Go thy ways; thou art as crooked a sprig as ever grew in
  London. I warrant him, he'll come to some naughty end or
  other, for his looks say no less. Besides, his father (you know,
  George) is none of the best; you heard him take me up like a
  flirt-gill, and sing bawdy songs upon me; but, i'faith, if I live,   20
  George—

CITIZEN
  Let me alone, sweetheart; I have a trick in my head shall
  lodge him in the Arches for one year, and make him sing
  peccavi ere I leave him, and yet he shall never know who
  hurt him neither.   25

WIFE
  Do, my good George, do.

                [Enter a BOY]

CITIZEN
  What shall we have Rafe do now, boy?

BOY
  You shall have what you will, sir.

20 *flirt-gill* wanton
23–4 *sing peccavi* pay a heavy penance ('*peccavi*', Latin 'I have sinned')

11–12 *hope . . . anchor.* An anchor sometimes appeared in emblems depicting
    hope; see A. Henkel and A. Schöne, *Emblemata* (Stuttgart, 1967),
    col. 1559.
15 *powers . . . celestial.* A reference to the Neo-Platonic figure of Venus
    Coelestis (Heavenly Love) who possesses the minds of honourable
    men whose intellects pass beyond the sphere of the senses towards
    heavenly things; see Erwin Panofsky, *Studies in Iconology* (Oxford,
    1939), pp. 142–3.
23 *Arches.* The Ecclesiastical Court of Appeal for the Province of Canter-
    bury that sat in the Church of St Mary de Arcubus in Cheapside. 'It
    took cognizance of all matters coming under Ecclesiastical Law, such
    as marriage and divorce, wills, abuses in the Church etc.' (Sugden).
    The Citizen infers that there was a prison attached to the Court.

CITIZEN

Why, so, sir; go and fetch me him then, and let the Sophy of
Persia come and christen him a child.   30

BOY

Believe me, sir, that will not do so well. 'Tis stale; it has
been had before at the Red Bull.

WIFE

George, let Rafe travel over great hills, and let him be very
weary, and come to the King of Cracovia's house, covered
with black velvet, and there let the king's daughter stand in   35
her window all in beaten gold, combing her golden locks
with a comb of ivory, and let her spy Rafe, and fall in love
with him, and come down to him, and carry him into her
father's house, and then let Rafe talk with her.

CITIZEN

Well said, Nell, it shall be so.—Boy, let's ha't done quickly.   40

BOY

Sir, if you will imagine all this to be done already, you shall
hear them talk together. But we cannot present a house
covered with black velvet, and a lady in beaten gold.

CITIZEN

Sir boy, let's ha't as you can, then.

BOY

Besides, it will show ill-favouredly to have a grocer's prentice   45
to court a king's daughter.

CITIZEN

Will it so, sir? You are well read in histories! I pray you, what
was Sir Dagonet? Was not he prentice to a grocer in London?

35 *black* ed. (om. Q1)
45 *show ill-favouredly* seem unfitting

29–30 *Sophy . . . child.* The Sophy of Persia stands godfather to Robert
Sherley's child in the last scene of Day, Rowley, and Wilkins's *The Travels
of the Three English Brothers* (printed 1607) which had been acted at the
Red Bull, a popular theatre in Clerkenwell, built about 1605. The boy
sneers because spectacular plays of little worth (*The Travels* is a good
example) were presented there.

34 *Cracovia.* Cracow, the ancient capital of Poland.

34–7 *covered . . . ivory.* The Revels accounts for the romantic plays presented at Court reveal how extravagant some of the productions were.

48 *Sir Dagonet.* He was in fact King Arthur's fool; cf. Malory's *Morte
d'Arthur*, ix. 19. The Citizen probably knew Sir Dagonet from Arthur's
Show, an exhibition of archery at Mile End by London citizens who
assumed the arms and names of knights of the Round Table; see
2 Henry IV, III. ii, 73.

Read the play of *The Four Prentices of London*, where they
toss their pikes so. I pray you, fetch him in, sir, fetch him in.   50

BOY

It shall be done.—It is not our fault, gentlemen.   *Exit*

WIFE

Now we shall see fine doings, I warrant'ee, George. Oh, here
they come; how prettily the King of Cracovia's daughter is
dressed.

> *Enter* RAFE *and the* LADY [POMPIONA], [TIM *as*] *Squire
> and* [GEORGE *as*] *Dwarf*

CITIZEN

Ay, Nell, it is the fashion of that country, I warrant'ee.   55

LADY

Welcome, sir knight, unto my father's court,
King of Moldavia; unto me, Pompiona,
His daughter dear. But sure you do not like
Your entertainment, that will stay with us
No longer but a night.

RAFE   Damsel right fair,   60
I am on many sad adventures bound,
That call me forth into the wilderness;
Besides, my horse's back is something galled,
Which will enforce me ride a sober pace.
But many thanks, fair lady, be to you,   65
For using errant knight with courtesy.

LADY

But say, brave knight, what is your name and birth?

RAFE

My name is Rafe; I am an Englishman,
As true as steel, a hearty Englishman,
And prentice to a grocer in the Strand   70

---

63 *galled* sore from chafing
70 *Strand* Q2 strond Q1

---

49 *The Four Prentices of London.* In Heywood's play Eustace and Guy
'before entering upon a combat with each other, toss and catch their
pikes to prove their strength of arm' (Murch).
57 *Moldavia.* One of the Danubian provinces in what is now Roumania.
The Prince of Moldavia was with the Turkish Ambassador at the
English Court in November 1607.

By deed indent, of which I have one part.
But Fortune calling me to follow arms,
On me this holy order I did take
Of Burning Pestle, which in all men's eyes
I bear, confounding ladies' enemies.   75

LADY
Oft have I heard of your brave countrymen,
And fertile soil and store of wholesome food;
My father oft will tell me of a drink
In England found, and 'nipitato' called,
Which driveth all the sorrow from your hearts.   80

RAFE
Lady, 'tis true, you need not lay your lips
To better nipitato than there is.

LADY
And of a wild fowl he will often speak
Which 'powdered beef and mustard' callèd is.
For there have been great wars 'twixt us and you;   85
But truly, Rafe, it was not long of me.
Tell me then, Rafe, could you contented be
To wear a lady's favour in your shield?

RAFE
I am a knight of religious order,
And will not wear a favour of a lady's   90
That trusts in Antichrist and false traditions.

CITIZEN
Well said, Rafe, convert her if thou canst.

RAFE
Besides, I have a lady of my own
In merry England, for whose virtuous sake
I took these arms, and Susan is her name,   95
A cobbler's maid in Milk Street, whom I vow
Ne'er to forsake whilst life and pestle last.

---

79 *nipitato* prime ale
84 *powdered* salted
86 *long of* on account of

---

71 *deed indent*. Articles of agreement between master and prentice were
drawn up in duplicate on one document which was then divided along
an irregular line. The two parts could be proved genuine if their
edges matched exactly.

LADY

  Happy that cobbling dame, whoe'er she be,
  That for her own, dear Rafe, hath gotten thee;
  Unhappy I, that ne'er shall see the day   100
  To see thee more, that bear'st my heart away.

RAFE

  Lady, farewell; I needs must take my leave.

LADY

  Hard-hearted Rafe, that ladies dost deceive.

CITIZEN

  Hark thee, Rafe, there's money for thee; give something in
  the King of Cracovia's house; be not beholding to him.   105

RAFE

  Lady, before I go, I must remember
  Your father's officers, who, truth to tell,
  Have been about me very diligent.
  Hold up thy snowy hand, thou princely maid:
  There's twelve pence for your father's chamberlain;   110
  And another shilling for his cook,
  For, by my troth, the goose was roasted well;
  And twelve pence for your father's horse-keeper,
  For 'nointing my horse back; and for his butter,
  There is another shilling; to the maid   115
  That washed my boot-hose, there's an English groat;
  And twopence to the boy that wiped my boots;
  And last, fair lady, there is for yourself
  Threepence, to buy you pins at Bumbo Fair.

LADY

  Full many thanks; and I will keep them safe   120
  Till all the heads be off, for thy sake, Rafe.

RAFE

  Advance, my squire and dwarf; I cannot stay.

LADY

  Thou kill'st my heart in parting thus away.   *Exeunt*

---

  98 *cobbling* pun on cobble = bungle
116 *boot-hose* stockings covering the upper part of the leg often
    elaborately embroidered

---

117 *boots.* Were worn by gallants and would-be gentlemen.
119 *pins.* Elaborate pins were fashionable.
119 *Bumbo.* The word probably comes from the name of a drink made from
    rum, water, and nutmeg doubtless drunk at fairs.

WIFE

I commend Rafe yet that he will not stoop to a Cracovian.
There's properer women in London than any are there, iwis.   125
But here comes Master Humphrey and his love again now,
George.

CITIZEN

Ay, cony, peace.

Enter MERCHANT, HUMPHREY, LUCE, *and a* BOY
[LUCE *kneels*]

MERCHANT

Go, get you up; I will not be entreated.
And, gossip mine, I'll keep you sure hereafter   130
From gadding out again with boys and unthrifts.
Come, they are women's tears; I know your fashion.—
Go, sirrah, lock her in, and keep the key
Safe as you love your life.   *Exeunt* LUCE *and* BOY
          Now, my son Humphrey,
You may both rest assured of my love   135
In this, and reap your own desire.

HUMPHREY

I see this love you speak of, through your daughter,
Although the hole be little; and hereafter
Will yield the like in all I may, or can,
Fitting a Christian, and a gentleman.   140

MERCHANT

I do believe you, my good son, and thank you:
For 'twere an impudence to think you flattered.

HUMPHREY

It were indeed; but shall I tell you why?
I have been beaten twice about the lie.

MERCHANT

Well, son, no more of compliment. My daughter   145
Is yours again; appoint the time, and take her;
We'll have no stealing for it. I myself
And some few of our friends will see you married.

124 *stoop* submit
125 *properer* handsomer
129 *up* either from her knees or to her chamber
130 *gossip* female friend
131 *unthrifts* prodigals
134 s.d. *Exeunt* ed. *Exit* Q1
137 *daughter* to rhyme with hereafter
147 *We'll . . . it* we shall not be niggardly

HUMPHREY

I would you would, i'faith, for, be it known,
I ever was afraid to lie alone.   150

MERCHANT

Some three days hence, then.

HUMPHREY   Three days? Let me see:
'Tis somewhat of the most; yet I agree
Because I mean against the appointed day
To visit all my friends in new array.

Enter SERVANT

SERVANT

Sir, there's a gentlewoman without would speak with your   155
worship.

MERCHANT

What is she?

SERVANT

Sir, I asked her not.

MERCHANT

Bid her come in.   [*Exit* SERVANT]

Enter MISTRESS MERRYTHOUGHT *and* MICHAEL

MISTRESS MERRYTHOUGHT

Peace be to your worship. I come as a poor suitor to you, sir,   160
in the behalf of this child.

MERCHANT

Are you not wife to Merrythought?

MISTRESS MERRYTHOUGHT

Yes, truly; would I had ne'er seen his eyes! He has undone
me and himself and his children, and there he lives at home,
and sings and hoits and revels among his drunken com-   165
panions; but, I warrant you, where to get a penny to put
bread in his mouth he knows not and therefore, if it like
your worship, I would entreat your letter to the honest host
of the Bell in Waltham, that I may place my child under the
protection of his tapster, in some settled course of life.   170

MERCHANT

I'm glad the heavens have heard my prayers. Thy husband,
When I was ripe in sorrows, laughed at me;
Thy son, like an unthankful wretch, I having
Redeemed him from his fall and made him mine,

---

152 *of . . . most* over-long
153 *against* in expectation of
163 *He* Q3 ha Q1

To show his love again, first stole my daughter,   175
Then wronged this gentleman, and, last of all,
Gave me that grief had almost brought me down
Unto my grave, had not a stronger hand
Relieved my sorrows. Go, and weep as I did,
And be unpitied; for I here profess   180
An everlasting hate to all thy name.

MISTRESS MERRYTHOUGHT

Will you so, sir? How say you by that?—Come, Mick, let
him keep his wind to cool his porridge. We'll go to thy
nurse's, Mick; she knits stockings, boy, and we'll knit too,
boy, and be beholding to none of them all.   185

    Exeunt MICHAEL *and* MOTHER [MISTRESS MERRYTHOUGHT]

        Enter a BOY *with a letter*

BOY

Sir, I take it you are the master of this house.

MERCHANT

How then, boy?

BOY

Then to yourself, sir, comes this letter.

MERCHANT

From whom, my pretty boy?

BOY

From him that was your servant; but no more   190
Shall that name ever be, for he is dead:
Grief of your purchased anger broke his heart.
I saw him die, and from his hand received
This paper, with a charge to bring it hither;
Read it, and satisfy yourself in all.   195

           LETTER

MERCHANT [*reads*]

'Sir, that I have wronged your love, I must confess; in which
I have purchased to myself, besides mine own undoing, the
ill opinion of my friends. Let not your anger, good sir, outlive
me, but suffer me to rest in peace with your forgiveness; let
my body (if a dying man may so much prevail with you) be   200
brought to your daughter, that she may truly know my hot
flames are now buried, and, withal, receive a testimony of
the zeal I bore her virtue. Farewell for ever, and be ever
happy. Jasper.'
God's hand is great in this. I do forgive him;   205

183 *keep . . . porridge* (Tilley, W 422)
192 *purchased* incurred by his conduct

Yet I am glad he's quiet, where I hope
He will not bite again.—Boy, bring the body,
And let him have his will, if that be all.

BOY

'Tis here without, sir.

MERCHANT   So, sir, if you please,
You may conduct it in; I do not fear it.   210

HUMPHREY

I'll be your usher, boy, for though I say it,
He owed me something once, and well did pay it.   *Exeunt*

Enter LUCE *alone*

LUCE

If there be any punishment inflicted
Upon the miserable, more than yet I feel,
Let it together seize me, and at once   215
Press down my soul. I cannot bear the pain
Of these delaying tortures. Thou that art
The end of all, and the sweet rest of all,
Come, come, oh Death, bring me to thy peace,
And blot out all the memory I nourish   220
Both of my father and my cruel friend.
Oh wretched maid, still living to be wretched,
To be a say to Fortune in her changes,
And grow to number times and woes together!
How happy had I been, if, being born,   225
My grave had been my cradle.

Enter SERVANT

SERVANT   By your leave,
Young mistress, here's a boy hath brought a coffin.
What 'a would say, I know not, but your father
Charged me to give you notice. Here they come.   [*Exit*]

Enter two [CARRIER *and a* BOY] *bearing a coffin,* JASPER *in it*

LUCE

For me I hope 'tis come, and 'tis most welcome.   230

BOY

Fair mistress, let me not add greater grief
To that great store you have already. Jasper,

---

223 *say* <assay, object for testing
230 *hope* Q2 hop't Q1

229 s.d. *two.* More men are probably required—see IV, 2.

That whilst he lived was yours, now dead
And here enclosed, commanded me to bring
His body hither, and to crave a tear   235
From those fair eyes, though he deserved not pity,
To deck his funeral; for so he bid me
Tell her for whom he died.
LUCE   He shall have many.—
Good friends, depart a little, whilst I take
My leave of this dead man that once I lov'd: 240
                    Exeunt COFFIN CARRIER *and* BOY
Hold yet a little, life, and then I give thee
To thy first heavenly being. Oh, my friend!
Hast thou deceived me thus, and got before me?
I shall not long be after. But, believe me,
Thou wert too cruel, Jasper, 'gainst thyself   245
In punishing the fault I could have pardoned,
With so untimely death. Thou didst not wrong me,
But ever were most kind, most true, most loving;
And I the most unkind, most false, most cruel.
Didst thou but ask a tear? I'll give thee all,   250
Even all my eyes can pour down, all my sighs,
And all myself, before thou goest from me.
These are but sparing rites; but if thy soul
Be yet about this place, and can behold
And see what I prepare to deck thee with,   255
It shall go up, borne on the wings of peace,
And satisfied. First will I sing thy dirge,
Then kiss thy pale lips, and then die myself,
And fill one coffin and one grave together.

                          SONG
            Come you whose loves are dead,   260
                  And whiles I sing
                  Weep and wring
            Every hand, and every head
            Bind with cypress and sad yew;
            Ribands black and candles blue   265
            For him that was of men most true.

---

253 *These* ed. there Q1

264 *cypress and sad yew.* Also used as emblems of mourning in 'Come away,
     come away, death' in *Twelfth Night*, II. iv, 50 ff.
265 *blue* was the colour of constancy.

> *Come with heavy moaning,*
> *And on his grave*
> *Let him have*
> *Sacrifice of sighs and groaning;*   270
> *Let him have fair flowers enow,*
> *White and purple, green and yellow,*
> *For him that was of most men true.*

Thou sable cloth, sad cover of my joys,
I lift thee up, and thus I meet with death.   275

JASPER [*rising out of the coffin*]

And thus you meet the living.

LUCE   Save me, heaven!

JASPER

Nay, do not fly me, fair; I am no spirit;
Look better on me; do you know me yet?

LUCE

Oh, thou dear shadow of my friend.

JASPER   Dear substance;
I swear I am no shadow; feel my hand,   280
It is the same it was. I am your Jasper,
Your Jasper that's yet living, and yet loving.
Pardon my rash attempt, my foolish proof
I put in practice of your constancy;
For sooner should my sword have drunk my blood   285
And set my soul at liberty, than drawn
The least drop from that body; for which boldness
Doom me to anything: if death, I take it,
And willingly.

LUCE   This death I'll give you for it.
                                        [*Kisses him*]
So, now I am satisfied; you are no spirit,   290
But my own truest, truest, truest friend.
Why do you come thus to me?

JASPER   First to see you,
Then to convey you hence.

LUCE   It cannot be,
For I am locked up here and watched at all hours,
That 'tis impossible for me to 'scape.   295

JASPER

Nothing more possible. Within this coffin
Do you convey yourself; let me alone,

267 *moaning* ed. mourning Q1
280 *shadow* shade, departed spirit

I have the wits of twenty men about me.
Only I crave the shelter of your closet
A little, and then fear me not. Creep in,   300
That they may presently convey you hence.
Fear nothing, dearest love; I'll be your second.

> [LUCE *lies down in the coffin, and*
> JASPER *covers her with the cloth*]

Lie close, so; all goes well yet.—Boy.

> [*Enter* BOY *and* COFFIN CARRIER]

BOY   At hand, sir.
JASPER

Convey away the coffin, and be wary.
BOY

'Tis done already.
JASPER   Now must I go conjure.   305
> *Exit*

> *Enter* MERCHANT

MERCHANT

Boy, boy!
BOY

Your servant, sir.
MERCHANT

Do me this kindness, boy (hold, here's a crown): before thou
bury the body of this fellow, carry it to his old merry father,
and salute him from me, and bid him sing; he hath cause.   310
BOY

I will, sir.
MERCHANT

And then bring me word what he is in, and have another
crown; but do it truly. I have fitted him a bargain now will
vex him.
BOY

God bless your worship's health, sir.   315
MERCHANT

Farewell, boy.   *Exeunt*

> *Enter* MASTER MERRYTHOUGHT

300 *fear me not* do not fear for me
302 *second* support
305 *conjure* arrange my deceptions
313 *fitted* furnished with

WIFE

   Ah, old Merrythought, art thou there again? Let's hear some
   of thy songs.

OLD MERRYTHOUGHT [*sings*]
>   *Who can sing a merrier note*
>   *Than he that cannot change a groat?*   320

   Not a denier left, and yet my heart leaps. I do wonder yet,
   as old as I am, that any man will follow a trade, or serve, that
   may sing and laugh, and walk the streets. My wife and both
   my sons are I know not where; I have nothing left, nor know
   I how to come by meat to supper; yet am I merry still, for I   325
   know I shall find it upon the table at six o'clock. Therefore,
   hang thought. [*sings*]
>   *I would not be a serving man*
>   *To carry the cloak-bag still,*
>   *Nor would I be a falconer*   330
>   *The greedy hawks to fill;*
>   *But I would be in a good house,*
>   *And have a good master too,*
>   *But I would eat and drink of the best,*
>   *And no work would I do.*   335

   This is it that keeps life and soul together: mirth. This is
   the philosopher's stone that they write so much on, that keeps
   a man ever young.

                          Enter a BOY

BOY

   Sir, they say they know all your money is gone, and they
   will trust you for no more drink.   340

OLD MERRYTHOUGHT

   Will they not? Let 'em choose. The best is, I have mirth at
   home, and need not send abroad for that; let them keep their
   drink to themselves. [*sings*]
>   *For Jillian of Bury she dwells on a hill,*
>   *And she hath good beer and ale to sell,*   345
>   *And of good fellows she thinks no ill;*
>   *And thither will we go now, now, now, now,*
>   *And thither will we go now.*

321 *denier* French coin, a twelfth of a sou, hence a very small sum
328–35 song printed on four lines Q1–3, F
329 *cloak-bag* portmanteau

319–20 *Who can sing a merrier note.* This catch is given in Ravenscroft's
   Pammelia (1609), ed. Warlock (Oxford, 1928), p. 26. It was proverbial,
   Tilley, N249.

And when you have made a little stay,
You need not ask what is to pay,   350
But kiss your hostess and go your way;
And thither, etc.

Enter another BOY

2 BOY
Sir, I can get no bread for supper.

OLD MERRYTHOUGHT
Hang bread and supper! Let's preserve our mirth, and we
shall never feel hunger, I'll warrant you. Let's have a catch;   355
boy, follow me; come, sing this catch: [*they sing*]

Ho, ho, nobody at home!
Meat, nor drink, nor money ha' we none.
Fill the pot, Eedy,
Never more need I.   360

So, boys, enough; follow me; let's change our place and we
shall laugh afresh.   *Exeunt*

Finis Act 4

[Interlude IV]

WIFE
Let him go, George; 'a shall not have any countenance from
us, nor a good word from any i'th' company, if I may strike
stroke in't.

CITIZEN
No more 'a sha'not, love; but, Nell, I will have Rafe do a
very notable matter now, to the eternal honour and glory of   5
all grocers.—Sirrah, you there, boy! Can none of you hear?

[*Enter* BOY]

BOY
Sir, your pleasure.

---

355 *catch* song sung as a round
356 *sing this catch* these words are separated from the preceding
    'come' by a space of 12.5 mm. in Q1–2 and may have been
    intended as a stage direction
357–60 printed as prose in Q1–3, F
362 *Finis Act 4* Q1–3, F print below line 61 of following interlude
  1 *countenance* favour
  2–3 *strike stroke* have my say

357–60 *Ho, ho, nobody at home!* Another catch from *Pammelia*, ed. Warlock,
p. 12.

CITIZEN

Let Rafe come out on May Day in the morning, and speak
upon a conduit with all his scarfs about him, and his feathers
and his rings and his knacks.   10

BOY

Why, sir, you do not think of our plot. What will become of
that, then?

CITIZEN

Why, sir, I care not what become on't. I'll have him come out,
or I'll fetch him out myself. I'll have something done in
honour of the city. Besides, he hath been long enough upon   15
adventures. Bring him out quickly, or, if I come in amongst
you—

BOY

Well, sir, he shall come out. But if our play miscarry, sir,
you are like to pay for't.   *Exit* BOY

CITIZEN

Bring him away, then.   20

WIFE

This will be brave, i'faith; George, shall not he dance the
morris too for the credit of the Strand?

CITIZEN

No, sweetheart, it will be too much for the boy.

Enter RAFE

Oh, there he is, Nell; he's reasonable well in reparel, but he
has not rings enough.   25

RAFE

London, to thee I do present the merry month of May;
Let each true subject be content to hear me what I say:
For from the top of conduit head, as plainly may appear,
I will both tell my name to you and wherefore I came here.
My name is Rafe, by due descent though not ignoble I,   30
Yet far inferior to the flock of gracious grocery;
And by the common counsel of my fellows in the Strand,

9 *conduit* cistern, fountain
23 s.d. printed after l. 25 in Q1
26–61 printed in italics in Q1–3, F

8 *May Day*. For the classic account of May Day festivities see Stubbes's
 Anatomy of Abuses (1583), Ch. xiii.
9 *scarfs* etc. The accoutrements of Morris dancers.
26ff. The speech is written in old-fashioned 'fourteeners', used, for example,
 in the heroical romance *Clyomon and Clamydes* (1570?).
30 *My name is Rafe*. A parody of the speech by the Ghost of Don Andrea in
 Kyd's *Spanish Tragedy*, I. i, 5–7.

With guilded staff and crossed scarf, the May Lord here I
    stand.
Rejoice, oh English hearts, rejoice; rejoice, oh lovers dear;
Rejoice, oh city, town, and country; rejoice eke every shire.   35
For now the fragrant flowers do spring and spout in seemly
    sort,
The little birds do sit and sing, the lambs do make fine sport.
And now the birchen tree doth bud, that makes the schoolboy
    cry;
The morris rings while hobby-horse doth foot it feateously.
The lords and ladies now abroad for their disport and play,   40
Do kiss sometimes upon the grass, and sometimes in the hay.
Now butter with a leaf of sage is good to purge the blood;
Fly Venus and phlebotomy, for they are neither good.
Now little fish on tender stone begin to cast their bellies,
And sluggish snails, that erst were mute, do creep out of
    their shellies.
                                     45
The rumbling rivers now do warm for little boys to paddle,
The sturdy steed now goes to grass, and up they hang his
    saddle.
The heavy hart, the bellowing buck, the rascal, and the pricket,
Are now among the yeoman's peas, and leave the fearful
    thicket.
And be like them, oh you, I say, of this same noble town,   50
And lift aloft your velvet heads, and, slipping off your gown,

38 *birchen* the birch was used for flogging
39 *feateously* nimbly
44 *cast their bellies* spawn
45 *erst* formerly
48 *rascal* young or inferior deer of herd
48 *pricket* buck in its second year

---

39 *hobby-horse.* Hobby-horses featured in the May Day festivities and
  were one of the prime targets of the Puritan denunciations; see *Women
  Pleased*, IV. i.; cf. the lament 'The hobbyhorse is forgot' that appears
  in several plays of the period (see note in Arden edition of *Love's
  Labour's Lost*, III. i, 28).
42 *butter* was supposed to have medicinal properties in May.
43 *Venus.* Intercourse was thought to be, like blood letting (phlebotomy),
  a loss of 'spirit.'
45 *snails.* 'Snails were used in love divinations: they were set to crawl on
  the hearth, and were thought to mark in the ashes the initials of the
  lover's name', Brand ii. 553. There is no need to emend mute to
  'mewed' = 'confined'.
51 *velvet heads.* 'A sly allusion to the horns of the citizens' (Dyce). The
  new antlers of a deer are velvety.

With bells on legs and napkins clean unto your shoulders tied,
With scarfs and garters as you please, and 'Hey for our town'
    cried,
March out, and show your willing minds, by twenty and by
    twenty,
To Hogsdon or to Newington, where ale and cakes are plenty.   55
And let it ne'er be said for shame, that we the youths of
    London
Lay thrumming of our caps at home, and left our custom
    undone.
Up then, I say, both young and old, both man and maid
    a-maying,
With drums and guns that bounce aloud, and merry tabor
    playing!
Which to prolong, God save our king, and send his country
    peace,   60
And root out treason from the Land! And so, my friends, I
    cease.   [*Exit*]

[Act V]

Enter MERCHANT, *solus*

MERCHANT
  I will have no great store of company at the wedding: a
couple of neighbours and their wives; and we will have a
capon in stewed broth, with marrow, and a good piece of beef,
stuck with rosemary.

Enter JASPER, *his face mealed*

JASPER
  Forbear thy pains, fond man; it is too late.   5
MERCHANT
  Heaven bless me! Jasper?
JASPER   Ay, I am his ghost,
  Whom thou hast injured for his constant love,
Fond worldly wretch, who dost not understand

57 *thrumming . . . caps* decorating our caps with tassels = wasting
  time
57 *custom* wenching
59 *tabor* small drum
  Act V ed. Actus 5. Scœna prima Q1
4 s.d. *mealed* whitened with flour

---

55 Hogsdon was a district north of London, Newington a suburb south of
  Southwark; both were favourites places for afternoon excursions.

In death that true hearts cannot parted be.
First, know thy daughter is quite borne away   10
On wings of angels, through the liquid air,
To far out of thy reach, and never more
Shalt thou behold her face. But she and I
Will in another world enjoy our loves,
Where neither father's anger, poverty,   15
Nor any cross that troubles earthly men
Shall make us sever our united hearts.
And never shalt thou sit, or be alone
In any place, but I will visit thee
With ghastly looks, and put into thy mind   20
The great offences which thou didst to me.
When thou art at thy table with thy friends,
Merry in heart, and filled with swelling wine,
I'll come in midst of all thy pride and mirth,
Invisible to all men but thyself,   25
And whisper such a sad tale in thine ear
Shall make thee let the cup fall from thy hand,
And stand as mute and pale as Death itself.

MERCHANT
Forgive me, Jasper. Oh, what might I do,
Tell me, to satisfy thy troubled ghost?   30

JASPER
There is no means; too late thou think'st of this.

MERCHANT
But tell me what were best for me to do?

JASPER
Repent thy deed, and satisfy my father,
And beat fond Humphrey out of thy doors.   *Exit* JASPER

Enter HUMPHREY

WIFE
Look, George, his very ghost would have folks beaten.   35

HUMPHREY
Father, my bride is gone, fair Mistress Luce;
My soul's the fount of vengeance, mischief's sluice.

---

16 *cross* impediment

19ff. The passage recalls the visit of Banquo's Ghost to Macbeth.

MERCHANT
  Hence, fool, out of my sight with thy fond passion!
  Thou has undone me.   *[Beats him]*
HUMPHREY   Hold, my father dear,
  For Luce thy daughter's sake, that had no peer.   40

MERCHANT
  Thy father, fool? There's some blows more, begone!
  Jasper, I hope thy ghost be well appeased
  To see thy will performed. Now will I go
  To satisfy thy father for thy wrongs.   *Exit*

HUMPHREY
  What shall I do? I have been beaten twice,   45
  And Mistress Luce is gone. Help me, device!
  Since my true love is gone, I nevermore,
  Whilst I do live, upon the sky will pore;
  But in the dark will wear out my shoe soles
  In passion in Saint Faith's Church under Paul's.   *Exit*   50

WIFE
  George, call Rafe hither; if you love me, call Rafe hither. I
  have the bravest thing for him to do, George; prithee call
  him quickly.
CITIZEN
  Rafe, why Rafe, boy!

                         Enter RAFE

RAFE
  Here, sir.   55
CITIZEN
  Come hither, Rafe; come to thy mistress, boy.
WIFE
  Rafe, I would have thee call all the youths together in battle-
  ray, with drums, and guns, and flags, and march to Mile End
  in pompous fashion, and there exhort your soldiers to be
  merry and wise, and to keep their beards from burning, Rafe;   60

---

38 *passion* grief; *passion!* ed. passion Q1
52 *bravest* most splendid
59 *pompous* ceremonial

---

50 *Faith's Church.* 'At the West ende of this Iesus Chappell, vnder the
  Quire of Paules, also was a parrish Church of Saint Faith, commonly
  called S. Faith vnder Paul's', Stow, i. 329. Gallants used to promenade
  in the aisle of the cathedral above, so Humphrey has chosen a fitting
  retreat.

and then skirmish, and let your flags fly, and cry, 'Kill, kill,
kill'. My husband shall lend you his jerkin, Rafe, and there's
a scarf; for the rest, the house shall furnish you, and we'll
pay for't. Do it bravely, Rafe, and think before whom you
perform, and what person you represent.   65

RAFE

I warrant you, mistress, if I do it not for the honour of the
city and the credit of my master, let me never hope for
freedom.

WIFE

'Tis well spoken, i'faith. Go thy ways; thou art a spark indeed.

CITIZEN

Rafe, Rafe, double your files bravely, Rafe.   70

RAFE

I warrant you, sir.   *Exit* RAFE

CITIZEN

Let him look narrowly to his service; I shall take him else.
I was there myself a pikeman once in the hottest of the day,
wench; had my feather shot sheer away, the fringe of my pike
burnt off with powder, my pate broken with a scouring-stick,   75
and yet I thank God I am here.   *Drum within*

WIFE

Hark, George, the drums.

CITIZEN

Ran, tan, tan, tan; ran, tan. Oh, wench, an thou hadst but
seen little Ned of Aldgate, Drum-Ned, how he made it roar
again, and laid on like a tyrant, and then struck softly till the   80
ward came up, and then thundered again, and together we go.
'Sa, sa, sa, bounce', quoth the guns; 'Courage, my hearts',
quoth the captains; 'Saint George', quoth the pikemen; and
withal here they lay, and there they lay. And yet for all this I
am here, wench.   85

WIFE

Be thankful for it, George, for indeed 'tis wonderful.

63 *house* theatre
68 *freedom* rank of freeman in the Grocers' Guild
70 *double your files* combine your two ranks
72 *narrowly* closely
72 *service* manoeuvres
72 *take* reprehend
75 *scouring-stick* for cleaning out a gun
81 *ward* detachment of militia

80 *tyrant*. A stock character in the mystery plays (Herod is an example).

Enter RAFE *and his company, with drums and colours*

RAFE

March fair, my hearts! Lieutenant, beat the rear up.—
Ancient, let your colours fly; but have a great care of the
butchers' hooks at Whitechapel; they have been the death of
many a fair ancient.— Open your files that I may take a view   90
both of your persons and munition.—Sergeant, call a muster.

SERGEANT

A stand!—William Hamerton, pewterer!

HAMERTON

Here, captain.

RAFE

A corslet and a Spanish pike; 'tis well. Can you shake it with
a terror?   95

HAMERTON

I hope so, captain.

RAFE

Charge upon me. [HAMERTON *charges upon* RAFE] 'Tis with
the weakest. Put more strength, William Hamerton, more
strength. As you were again.—Proceed, Sergeant.

SERGEANT

George Greengoose, poulterer!   100

GREENGOOSE

Here.

RAFE

Let me see your piece, neighbour Greengoose; when was
she shot in?

GREENGOOSE

An't like you, master captain, I made a shot even now, partly
to scour her, and partly for audacity.   105

RAFE

It should seem so certainly, for her breath is yet inflamed;
besides, there is a main fault in the touch-hole, it runs and
stinketh; and I tell you moreover, and believe it, ten such
touch-holes would breed the pox in the army. Get you a

87 *beat . . . up* round up, stir up with a drum-roll
88 *Ancient* ensign-bearer
91 *muster* roll
94 *corslet* armour covering the body
102 *piece* firearm; the whole of this scene contains bawdy puns
104 *An't* ed. And Q1

89 *Whitechapel.* A parish east of Aldgate; there was a row of butchers'
shops along one side of the Whitechapel Road.

feather, neighbour, get you a feather, sweet oil, and paper,   110
and your piece may do well enough yet. Where's your
powder?

GREENGOOSE

Here.

RAFE

What, in a paper? As I am a soldier and a gentleman, it
craves a martial court. You ought to die for't. Where's your   115
horn? Answer me to that.

GREENGOOSE

An't like you, sir, I was oblivious.

RAFE

It likes me not you should be so; 'tis a shame for you, and a
scandal to all our neighbours, being a man of worth and
estimation, to leave your horn behind you: I am afraid 'twill   120
breed example. But let me tell you no more on't.—Stand,
till I view you all.—What's become o'th nose of your flask?

1 SOLDIER

Indeed la, captain, 'twas blown away with powder.

RAFE

Put on a new one at the city's charge.—Where's the stone of
this piece?   125

2 SOLDIER

The drummer took it out to light tobacco.

RAFE

'Tis a fault, my friend; put it in again.—You want a nose—
and you a stone.—Sergeant, take a note on't, for I mean to
stop it in the pay.—Remove, and march! Soft and fair,
gentlemen, soft and fair! Double your files! As you were!   130
Faces about! Now, you with the sodden face, keep in there!
Look to your match, sirrah, it will be in your fellow's flask
anon. So, make a crescent now; advance your pikes; stand,
and give ear! Gentlemen, countrymen, friends, and my
fellow-soldiers, I have brought you this day from the shops   135
of security and the counters of content, to measure out in
these furious fields honour by the ell, and prowess by the

116 *horn* powder horn and cuckold's horn
117 *oblivious* forgetful
124 *stone* flint
127 *want* lack
137 *ell* a measure of 45 inches.

134ff. Rafe's exhortation to his soldiers contains echoes of Richard III's
    oration to his army, V. iii, 313 ff.

pound. Let it not, oh, let it not, I say, be told hereafter the
noble issue of this city fainted, but bear yourselves in this
fair action like men, valiant men, and freemen. Fear not the   140
face of the enemy, nor the noise of the guns, for believe me,
brethren, the rude rumbling of a brewer's car is far more
terrible, of which you have a daily experience; neither let the
stink of powder offend you, since a more valiant stink is
nightly with you. To a resolved mind his home is everywhere.   145
I speak not this to take away the hope of your return; for you
shall see, I do not doubt it, and that very shortly, your loving
wives again, and your sweet children, whose care doth bear
you company in baskets. Remember, then, whose cause you
have in hand, and like a sort of true-born scavengers, scour   150
me this famous realm of enemies. I have no more to say but
this: stand to your tacklings, lads, and show to the world
you can as well brandish a sword as shake an apron. Saint
George, and on, my hearts!

OMNES
Saint George! Saint George!   *Exeunt*   155

WIFE
'Twas well done, Rafe. I'll send thee a cold capon a-field,
and a bottle of March beer; and it may be, come myself to
see thee.

CITIZEN
Nell, the boy has deceived me much; I did not think it had
been in him. He has performed such a matter, wench, that   160
if I live, next year I'll have him captain of the galley-foist, or
I'll want my will.

               Enter OLD MERRYTHOUGHT

OLD MERRYTHOUGHT
Yet, I thank God, I break not a wrinkle more than I had.
Not a stoup, boys? Care live with cats, I defy thee! My
heart is as sound as an oak; and though I want drink to wet   165
my whistle, I can sing [*sings*]:

148–9 *whose . . . baskets* who show their care by sending you provisions
150 *sort* company
152 *tacklings* weapons (with a bawdy sense)
157 *March beer* strong beer
161 *galley-foist* state barge of the Lord Mayor
163 *break* show
164 *stoup* a measure of liquor, two quarts
164 *Care . . cats* cf. 'Care will kill a cat' (Tilley, C 84)

Come no more there, boys, come no more there;
For we shall never whilst we live, come any more there.

Enter a BOY [*and* COFFIN-CARRIERS] *with a Coffin*

BOY
    God save you, sir.
OLD MERRYTHOUGHT
    It's a brave boy. Canst thou sing?   170
BOY
    Yes, sir, I can sing, but 'tis not so necessary at this time.
OLD MERRYTHOUGHT [*sings*]
            Sing we, and chant it,
            Whilst love doth grant it.
BOY
    Sir, sir, if you knew what I have brought you, you would
    have little list to sing.   175
OLD MERRYTHOUGHT [*sings*]
            Oh, the minion round,
            Full long I have thee sought,
            And now I have thee found,
            And what hast thou here brought?
BOY
    A coffin, sir, and your dead son Jasper in it.   180
OLD MERRYTHOUGHT
    Dead? [*sings*]
            Why, farewell he.
            Thou wast a bonny boy,
            And I did love thee.

Enter JASPER

JASPER
    Then, I pray you, sir, do so still.   185
OLD MERRYTHOUGHT
    Jasper's ghost? [*sings*]
        Thou art welcome from Stygian lake so soon;
        Declare to me what wondrous things in Pluto's court are done.
JASPER
    By my troth, sir, I ne'er came there; 'tis too hot for me, sir.

176 *minion* ed. Mimon Q1
177 *long* Q2 long long Q1

172–3 *Sing we, and chant it.* Words and music in Thomas Morley's *Ballets
    to Five Voices* (*1595 and 1600*), ed. E. H. Fellowes (London, 1913),
    No. 4.

OLD MERRYTHOUGHT
   A merry ghost, a very merry ghost! [*sings*]   190
     And where is your true love? Oh, where is yours?

JASPER
   Marry, look you, sir.
             Heaves up the Coffin, [and LUCE *climbs out]*

OLD MERRYTHOUGHT
   Ah, ha! Art thou good at that, i'faith?   [*sings*]
       With hey, trixy, terlery-whiskin,
         The world it runs on wheels,   195
       When the young man's — —,
         Up goes the maiden's heels.

      MISTRESS MERRYTHOUGHT *and* MICHAEL *within*

MISTRESS MERRYTHOUGHT [*within*]
   What, Master Merrythought, will you not let's in? What do
   you think shall become of us?

OLD MERRYTHOUGHT
   What voice is that that calleth at our door?   200

MISTRESS MERRYTHOUGHT [*within*]
   You know me well enough; I am sure I have not been such
   a stranger to you.

OLD MERRYTHOUGHT [*sings*]
       And some they whistled, and some they sung,
         Hey, down, down!
       And some did loudly say,   205
       Ever as the Lord Barnet's horn blew,
         Away, Musgrave, away.

MISTRESS MERRYTHOUGHT [*within*]
   You will not have us starve here, will you, Master Merrythought?

JASPER
   Nay, good sir, be persuaded, she is my mother. If her   210
   offences have been great against you, let your own love
   remember she is yours, and so forgive her.

LUCE
   Good Master Merrythought, let me entreat you; I will not
   be denied.

---

195 *world . . . wheels* (Tilley, W 893)

203–7 *And some they whistled, and some they sung.* From the ballad of
   Little Musgrave and Lady Barnard; Child No. 81, music in Bronson,
   ii. 267 ff.

MISTRESS MERRYTHOUGHT [*within*]
   Why, Master Merrythought, will you be a vexed thing still?   215
OLD MERRYTHOUGHT
   Woman, I take you to my love again; but you shall sing
before you enter; therefore dispatch your song and so come in.
MISTRESS MERRYTHOUGHT [*within*]
   Well, you must have your will when all's done.—Mick, what
song canst thou sing, boy?
MICHAEL
   I can sing none, forsooth, but 'A Lady's Daughter of Paris'   220
properly.
MISTRESS MERRYTHOUGHT [*and* MICHAEL]
            SONG
      It was a lady's daughter, etc.

   [OLD MERRYTHOUGHT *admits* MISTRESS MERRYTHOUGHT
          and MICHAEL]

OLD MERRYTHOUGHT
   Come, you're welcome home again. [*sings*]
      If such danger be in playing,
      And jest must to earnest turn,   225
      You shall go no more a-maying.
MERCHANT [*within*]
   Are you within, sir? Master Merrythought?
JASPER
   It is my master's voice. Good sir, go hold him in talk, whilst
we convey ourselves into some inward room.
                      [*Exit with* LUCE]

---

215 *vexed* cantankerous

---

222 *It was a lady's daughter.* From a broadside ballad that begins:

       It was a lady's daughter,
         Of Paris properly,
       Her mother her commanded
         To mass that she should hie:
       O pardon me, dear mother,
         Her daughter dear did say,
       Unto that filthy idol
         I never can obey.

   It is printed in *The Roxburghe Ballads* (ed. 1896), Vol. I, part I, pp.
35–7.
224–6 *If such danger be in playing.* The refrain of 'My Love hath vowed'
   from Philip Rosseter's *Book of Ayres* (1601), No. 5; it is reprinted in
   E. H. Fellowes's *English Madrigal Verse, 1588–1632* (3rd edition,
   Oxford, 1967), p. 656.

OLD MERRYTHOUGHT
    What are you? Are you merry? You must be very merry if   230
    you enter.
MERCHANT [*within*]
    I am, sir.
OLD MERRYTHOUGHT
    Sing then.
MERCHANT [*within*]
    Nay, good sir, open to me.
OLD MERRYTHOUGHT
    Sing, I say, or, by the merry heart, you come not in.   235
MERCHANT [*within*]
    Well, sir, I'll sing: [*sings*]
                    Fortune my foe, etc.

        [OLD MERRYTHOUGHT *admits* MERCHANT]

OLD MERRYTHOUGHT
    You are welcome, sir, you are welcome. You see your
    entertainment; pray you, be merry.
MERCHANT
    Oh, Master Merrythought, I am come to ask you   240
    Forgiveness for the wrongs I offered you
    And your most virtuous son; they're infinite;
    Yet my contrition shall be more than they.
    I do confess my hardness broke his heart,
    For which just heaven hath given me punishment   245
    More than my age can carry. His wandering spirit,
    Not yet at rest, pursues me everywhere,
    Crying, 'I'll haunt thee for thy cruelty'.
    My daughter, she is gone, I know not how,
    Taken invisible, and whether living   250
    Or in grave, 'tis yet uncertain to me.
    Oh Master Merrythought, these are the weights
    Will sink me to my grave. Forgive me, sir.

---

237 *Fortune my foe.* One of the most popular songs of the period; the
    first stanza is:

            Fortune my foe, why dost thou frown on me?
            And will thy favours never better be?
            Wilt thou, I say, for ever breed my pain?
            And wilt thou not restore my joys again?

    words and music in Chappell, i. 76.

OLD MERRYTHOUGHT
  Why, sir, I do forgive you, and be merry;
  And if the wag in's lifetime played the knave,   255
  Can you forgive him too?
MERCHANT   With all my heart, sir.
OLD MERRYTHOUGHT
  Speak it again, and heartily.
MERCHANT   I do, sir,
  Now, by my soul, I do.
OLD MERRYTHOUGHT [sings]
      With that came out his paramour;
      She was as white as the lily flower,   260
      Hey, trolly, trolly, lolly.

                  Enter LUCE *and* JASPER

      With that came out her own dear knight,
      He was as true as ever did fight. etc.
  Sir, if you will forgive 'em, clap their hands together; there's
  no more to be said i'th' matter.   265
MERCHANT
  I do, I do.

CITIZEN
  I do not like this.—Peace, boys, hear me one of you. Every-
  body's part is come to an end but Rafe's, and he's left out.
BOY
  'Tis long of yourself, sir; we have nothing to do with his part.
CITIZEN
  Rafe, come away.—Make an end on him as you have done of   270
  the rest, boys; come.
WIFE
  Now, good husband, let him come out and die.
CITIZEN
  He shall Nell.—Rafe, come away quickly and die, boy.
BOY
  'Twill be very unfit he should die, sir, upon no occasion, and
  in a comedy too.   275

264 *clap* strike hands together in token of betrothal
265 *said* Q2 sad Q1
270 *an end* ed. (om. Q1)

CITIZEN
> Take you no care of that, sir boy, is not his part at an end,
> think you, when he's dead?—Come away, Rafe.

Enter RAFE, *with a forked arrow through his head*

RAFE
> When I was mortal, this my costive corpse
> Did lap up figs and raisins in the Strand,
> Where sitting, I espied a lovely dame,   280
> Whose master wrought with lingel and with awl,
> And under ground he vamped many a boot.
> Straight did her love prick forth me, tender sprig,
> To follow feats of arms in warlike wise
> Through Waltham Desert, where I did perform   285
> Many achievements, and did lay on ground
> Huge Barbaroso, that insulting giant,
> And all his captives soon set at liberty.
> Then honour pricked me from my native soil
> Into Moldavia, where I gained the love   290
> Of Pompiona, his beloved daughter,
> But yet proved constant to the black-thumbed maid
> Susan, and scorned Pompiona's love.
> Yet liberal I was, and gave her pins,
> And money for her father's officers.   295
> I then returned home, and thrust myself
> In action, and by all men chosen was
> Lord of the May, where I did flourish it,
> With scarfs and rings, and posy in my hand.
> After this action, I preferred was,   300
> And chosen city captain at Mile End,
> With hat and feather and with leading-staff,

277 s.d. *forked* barbed
281 *lingel* shoemaker's waxed thread
282 *vamped* renewed the uppers of
287 *insulting* bragging
291 *his* the King of Moldavia's
299 *posy* Q1ᶜ Poesie Q1ᵘ; a motto inscribed in a ring
302 *leading-staff* officer's baton

---

277 s.d. Cf. the s.d. in *The True Tragedy of Richard Duke of York* (1595):
   'Enter Clifford wounded, with an arrow in his necke'.
278ff. The speech parodies ghost scenes from several plays, including
   Henry VI to Richard (*Richard III*, V. iii, 124), and the beginning of
   The Spanish Tragedy; it also contains echoes of Quicksilver's 'Repen-
   tance' in *Eastward Ho* (1605), V. v, 49 ff.

And trained my men and brought them all off clear
(Save one man that berayed him with the noise).
But all these things I Rafe did undertake   305
Only for my beloved Susan's sake.
Then coming home, and sitting in my shop
With apron blue, Death came unto my stall
To cheapen *aqua vitae;* but ere I
Could take the bottle down, and fill a taste,   310
Death caught a pound of pepper in his hand,
And sprinkled all my face and body o'er,
And in an instant vanished away.

CITIZEN
'Tis a pretty fiction i'faith.

RAFE
Then took I up my bow and shaft in hand,   315
And walked into Moorfields to cool myself;
But there grim cruel Death met me again,
And shot this forked arrow through my head,
And now I faint. Therefore be warned by me,
My fellows every one, of forked heads.   320
Farewell, all you good boys in merry London;
Ne'er shall we more upon Shrove Tuesday meet
And pluck down houses of iniquity.
My pain increaseth.—I shall never more
Hold open, whilst another pumps both legs,   325

304 *berayed him* befouled himself
309 *cheapen* bargain for
320 *forked heads* of cuckolds

---

316 *Moorfields*. North of the city wall, between Bishopsgate and Cripplegate; in 1606 they were laid out in walks and became a popular summer resort for the citizens.
322 *Shrove Tuesday*. The prentices traditionally revelled and rioted on Shrove Tuesday before Lent; see Brand, ii. 53 ff.; *The Shoemakers' Holiday, passim*; and John Taylor's *Iack a Lent* (London, 1620), Sig. B2ᵛ: 'Then these Youths . . . put play-houses to the sack, and Bawdy-houses to the spoil, in the quarrel breaking a thousand quarrels (of glasse I meane) making ambitious brickbats breake their necks, tumbling from the tops of lofty chimnies' etc.
325 *Hold . . . legs*. Dr Craik compares the Induction to *Bartholomew Fair*: 'would not a fine pump upon the stage ha' done well for a property now? and a punk set under upon her head, with her stern upward, and ha' been sous'd by my witty young masters o' the Inns o' Court'.

Nor daub a satin gown with rotten eggs;
Set up a stake, oh, never more I shall.
I die; fly, fly, my soul, to Grocers' Hall.
Oh, oh, oh, etc.

WIFE

Well said, Rafe. Do your obeisance to the gentlemen and go   330
your ways. Well said, Rafe.   *Exit* RAFE

OLD MERRYTHOUGHT

Methinks all we, thus kindly and unexpectedly reconciled,
should not depart without a song.

MERCHANT

A good motion.

OLD MERRYTHOUGHT

Strike up, then.   335

SONG

> *Better music ne'er was known*
> *Than a choir of hearts in one.*
> *Let each other that hath been*
> *Troubled with the gall or spleen,*
> *Learn of us to keep his brow*   340
> *Smooth and plain as ours are now.*
> *Sing, though before the hour of dying;*
> *He shall rise, and then be crying,*
> *'Hey, ho, 'tis nought but mirth,*
> *That keeps the body from the earth'.*   345
>   *Exeunt* OMNES

Epilogus

CITIZEN

Come Nell, shall we go? The play's done.

WIFE

Nay, by my faith, George, I have more manners than so; I'll
speak to these gentlemen first.—I thank you all, gentlemen,
for your patience and countenance to Rafe, a poor fatherless
child; and if I might see you at my house, it should go hard   5
but I would have a pottle of wine and a pipe of tobacco for

333 *depart* take leave of one another
 6 *pottle* measure of two quarts

---

327 *Set up a stake*. 'Rafe probably refers to the stake to which cocks were
tied as targets to be thrown at in the contests on Shrove Tuesday'
(Murch).

you; for, truly, I hope you do like the youth, but I would be glad to know the truth. I refer it to your own discretions, whether you will applaud him or no; for I will wink, and whilst you shall do what you will. I thank you with all my heart. God give you good night.—Come, George.   10

FINIS

9 *wink* close my eyes
10 *whilst* meanwhile